FAMILY
PASTORAL
CARE

SUCCESSFUL PASTORAL COUNSELING SERIES

VOLUMES PUBLISHED

Principles and Practices of Pastoral Care, by Dr. Russell L. Dicks

Ministering to the Physically Sick, by Dr. Carl J. Scherzer

Helping the Alcoholic and His Family, by Dr. Thomas J. Shipp

Marital Counseling, by Dr. R. Lofton Hudson

Counseling the Childless Couple, by The Reverend William T. Bassett

Premarital Guidance, by Dr. Russell L. Dicks

Ministering to the Dying, by Carl J. Scherzer

Ministering to Deeply Troubled People, by Dr. Ernest E. Bruder

Theology and Pastoral Counseling, by Dr. Edward E. Thornton

Group Counseling, by Dr. Joseph W. Knowles

Ministering to the Grief Sufferer, by Dr. C. Charles Bachmann

Counseling with Senior Citizens, by The Reverend J. Paul Brown

Counseling the Serviceman and His Family, by Chaplain Thomas A. Harris

Counseling the Unwed Mother, by The Reverend Helen E. Terkelsen

Counseling with College Students, by Dr. Charles F. Kemp

Preaching and Pastoral Care, by Dr. Arthur L. Teikmanis

Helping Youth in Conflict, by The Reverend Francis I. Frellick

Understanding and Helping the Narcotic Addict, by Tommie L. Duncan

Counseling with Teen-Agers, by The Reverend Robert A. Blees and Staff of First Community Church

Psychiatry and Pastoral Care, by Edgar Draper, M.D.

Family Pastoral Care, by Dr. Russell J. Becker

Depth Perspectives in Pastoral Work, by Thomas W. Klink

VOLUMES IN PREPARATION

Ministering to Prisoners and Their Families, by Dr. Henry H. Cassler

Referral in Pastoral Counseling, by Dr. William B. Oglesby, Jr.

FAMILY PASTORAL CARE

RUSSELL J. BECKER

PRENTICE-HALL, INC., ENGLEWOOD CLIFFS, N.J.

To my two families of mutual care—
one with a mother, a father and ten
other children which fitted me for the
other with Dorothy and our boys, Jonathan,
Carl and Kurt

INTRODUCTION

This series of books represents the most comprehensive publishing effort ever made in the field of pastoral care. These books could not have been published twenty-five years ago or probably even ten, for the material was not then available. In the past, single books have been available covering different phases of the task. Now we are bringing the subjects together in a single series. Here we present a library of pastoral care covering the major topics and problems that most pastors will encounter in their ministry. Fortunately, not all of these problems need be faced every week or even every month. But, when they are, the minister wants help and he wants it immediately.

These books are prepared for the nonspecialized minister serving the local church, where he is the most accessible professional person in the community. It is a well-accepted fact that more people turn to clergy when in trouble than to all other professional people. Therefore, the pastor must not fail them.

Russell L. Dicks
General Editor

This book is a reflection of parish work in spite of the fact that the author has been on a theological faculty the last five years. As a statement from the parish what is written should be taken as a contribution to professional conversation. A point of view is presented to which I hope others will respond creatively and imaginatively in their own parish situations.

In part one the point is stressed that there is a significant ministry of the *laity* in pastoral care. I try to suggest one such area of the lay ministry in pastoral care which has great bearing on the issues confronting the family in our changing society. The small group gathered in Christ is a means of equipping the saints for their work of pastoral ministry to each other. This ministry of mutual care has much to contribute to the crises in family life today. A consequence of this point of view is a changed view of the ministry of the minister. He is lifted from the role of *the* pastoral counselor into the role of a pastor to pastors. Implicit in this approach is a view of the church as a ministering community and a missionary body in the world. Believers in Christ serve and strengthen one another within the fellowship so that they may go forth into the world and render service to the one who is Lord. Many members of the Glenview (Illinois) Community Church contributed greatly to the venture in mutual pastoral care reported here. In its mutuality they ministered to their shepherds as well as to each other. For this I express my gratitude.

In part two the approach to family counseling advocated is very brief in its time demands. The brevity of time involved is based on the assumption that not every family disturbance is a deep neurotic struggle. When family difficulty can be seen as a skewing

of role relationships, then the clarification of roles will have a recti-
fying effect upon the disturbance within the family constellation.
The distinguishing feature of the presentation made is the use of
a full verbatim transcript of an actual family counseling session.

Allowing a full transcript of a recorded family counseling session
to go forth into print and tape reproduction is not an easy matter
either for the family involved or for the counselor. Let me acknowledge with appreciation here the generous consent of this family to
having their time of stress made visible and audible to others. Their
anonymity or pseudonymity protects privacy while offering something of value to others. They make their gift with the hope that
this may help others in their ministries to families. Other families
may find this case material personally helpful just in reading it.
Such was the case for the Betterlys as they reviewed the typescript
prior to publication.

While this book is intended as a handbook for the working pastor
who already has some familiarity with the general principles of
pastoral care, it is my hope that laymen will read it with profit.
Chapter Two on the lay ministry in pastoral care should properly be
considered a guide to the layman as well as to pastors. The material of the fully recorded family counseling session in Chapters Five
and Six should prove beneficial in its own content—apart from
the technical concerns of a family counseling approach—to all who
live in families.

The general approach of the author in counseling work is deeply
influenced by a half dozen years of study and work with Carl R.
Rogers. At the same time I am convinced that the requirements of
pastoral care mean "throwing the book away" at times and dealing
creatively with the confronting situation. Such is the temper of the
section on family counseling. Beyond the wisdom derived from
worldly shepherds such as Carl R. Rogers is, there is a firm commitment to the *pastoral* distinctions in pastoral care. This point of
view takes seriously the message of our redemption in Jesus Christ.
At the same time it addresses with realism the social and psychological realities of the lives of people and utilizes disciplines of the
behavioral sciences for analysis and understanding. In addition, the
church and ministry as the bearers of and witnesses to God's Word

of our redemption are taken as the arena of our continuing encounter with that Word.

I hope the point of view I hold is psychologically, pastorally and theologically informed in each instance of ministry.

Russell J. Becker

CONTENTS

Preface 6

Part I

CONGREGATIONAL CARE WITH FAMILIES

1. The Family under Stress 13
2. Congregational Care 33

Part II

FAMILY COUNSELING

3. Persons in Families 65
4. An Approach to Family Counseling 75
5. A Family Counseling Session (Part I) 87
6. A Family Counseling Session (Part II) 114
   A Pastoral Theological Postscript 132
   A Selected Bibliography 137
   Index 143

Part I

CONGREGATIONAL CARE WITH FAMILIES

CHAPTER ONE

The FAMILY Under STRESS

Pastoral Care to the family is a form of the ministry of Christ which is shaped by the Gospel as a message of reconciliation, by the church as a community of belief and love, by a ministry which equips the "saints" for their work of ministry and by an understanding of the family as a human group within society. The meaning of the Gospel as a formative and shaping reality upon pastoral care has been too little acknowledged in the contemporary field of pastoral care in America. Full attention to this is the subject of a theology of pastoral care.[1] Of necessity this is one of the secondary concerns of this volume. The meaning of the church and some of its new structures for ministry will be dealt with later.

Consider the place of the family in American society today. A ministry, however well informed by Gospel and ecclesiology, requires full understanding of the persons to whom it is directed. In looking at the family our perspective, while sociologically informed, is not simply that of the sociologist. Beyond the descriptive task we take the pastoral work of ministry with primary seriousness. We therefore are interested in the critical points in the life of the family. We wish to assess not simply what is happening to the family today, but where are the issues which are decisive for stability or distress within the family. We seek those points which might help us to give focus and direction to the intensive ministry to the family today.

The family we shall be considering is the urban-suburban middle-

---

[1] See *Theology and Pastoral Counseling* by Edward E. Thornton in this series (72).

class family. The family in its isolated rural or in its compacted, inner city forms admittedly will manifest important variations or exceptions to some of what follows.

The Crisis of Intimacy

The separation of work and home.   The industrial revolution has been with us a long time now, so that the effects of the separation of work and residence are not new. What is new in this century is the fact that urbanization has galloped forward at such a pace that fewer than one-twelfth of the families still live on farms. And this number is narrowing rapidly. The predominant fact about the family is no longer its rural, agrarian place but its urban or suburban locale. In the metropolis the place where the breadwinner works and where he "lives" are separated. So separate are these spheres that one of the important pressures upon the family accumulates because of this primary fact. The husband and wife live in separate worlds.

Listen to the complaint of one suburban housewife and mother of three small children about her husband's separate world:

> How any person can be among adults and going some place and at some place and coming home and not see or hear a single interesting thing is something I can't understand, because if ever I'm with people or going some place I see things and want to talk about them! And here is Jim gone all day and comes home and has absolutely nothing to say! I've gotten to the point where I just believe he has nothing to say and is not holding back.

The world of contracts, sales negotiations with other countries, reorganization of the company through merger with a larger company are some of the preoccupations of this woman's lawyer-husband at his work. But when he comes home he wants rest. He also finds tumbling children, household pandemonium, school interests of the child's day, neighbor stresses of the wife's day and the squabbles she faces in the church woman's group. Out of a sense of chivalry and recognition that his wife has already had about enough to cope with, he may spare her the bruises and scars of his battles that day. She may also be desirous of making her home a haven and a place of rest for her harried husband and engage in some chivalrous silence as well. The worlds stay apart either way.

Or consider the lament of another husband:

What am I to say when I meet my wife? "Well, the computer program today was jammed in one of its loops with no monitor clue." She wouldn't have the slightest idea what I was talking about.

This points to the fact that technical specialization is developing at such a pace that this too is driving a wedge between the world of the wife and the husband's world. It is a wedge which shows itself in any social gathering of couples in which the men gather to engage in talk about the world of business and women cluster to discuss children.

The isolated conjugal family. Another factor which contributes to the crisis of intimacy is the changed definition of the family which holds in our society. There was a time when the family included several generations of adults and various spinster aunts joined in an economic unit which was also a powerful unit of human association. The extended family is no longer an economic necessity and it is not desired as a form of human association. To identify the isolated husband and wife as the family unit the sociologist speaks of the conjugal family. Marriage defines a family whether children come along or not, whether they are still present or not. When children come along they will know intimately only their immediate parents. The separation of parental generations is normative in America today.

The economic necessities of a fluid, changing, technical manufacturing world require highly mobile families. Extended families tend to become rooted. They become soil-dominated. Changing work positions to meet changing opportunities can occur only if the family is ready to pack up and move. Ready we are. Frequently all that a family considers really important is that which it packs into a moving van. The moving van symbolizes the contemporary family the way a homestead once did. The family, so far as persons are concerned, are the husband and wife with children and dog who follow the moving van wherever it leads. It leads one family in five across county lines every year. The family inside that car, following the moving van to its next home is cut off from grandparents and relatives of every kind. It is rootless in its new community. Husbands and wives, parents and children, are turned in upon each other for expressions of intimacy. The isolated conjugal family is expected to provide the emotional well-springs of living for each member. The intensity of this demand can be sensed by taking the family in the car following the moving van as a paradigm of what it is when it unpacks in its next home. Or the family living in the house on wheels, the house trailer, as five million American families now do, is the paradigm of family life today. It is not just the physical close-quarters which is crucial. It is the fact that only a very few people are expected to enter intimately into the life of another person.

If the self in an interpersonal sense is a creative product of the other selves which enter into its own existence as a part of its own being, then the isolated, conjugal family unit is asking that virtually all the humanity which feeds the young child comes from the interaction of a very small circle of people. The pressure upon the family to produce emotionally sound and healthy personalities for a complexly interdependent society which has low tolerance for psychic deviations is a pressure of critical dimensions. Obviously we are failing miserably in the segment of society which does not share in the rewards of a productive economy. The incidence of serious mental illness among the lowest socio-economic groups in our society is ten times more frequent than among the middle and upper classes. (2, 3) At the same time the studies which reveal this to us reveal that the middle-class family by and large is meeting the requirements of good emotional development with a fair degree of success. In a broad sense, there is no cause for alarm over the inward and narrow intimacy orientation of the isolated, conjugal family. At the same time, there is a socially structured pressure here. The isolated, conjugal family needs each of its few members for the important work of interpersonal development especially for its younger members. Cut off from grandparents and other relatives with their contributions of love and concern to the well being of the family members, cut off by frequent mobility from meaningful associations among neighbors, the family today can ill afford the breadwinner who turns toward the office or factory as a center of affective reality for his life. When this happens a crisis is at hand. The affective reserves against disastrous loss are low. The isolated, conjugal family risks a significant emotional loss when the breadwinner spends the most important part of his day away from the home. The working-class family fares better here than the executive, managerial, professional family. The combination of limited work hours and drab repetitiveness in assembly production tends to make the working-class father both available to his family and more interested in them than his work. For the professional and managerial groups in our society both interesting work and long hours draw such a father out of his family. He becomes the *pater absconditus,* the hidden father. It leaves an even smaller circle in which intimacy needs must be met. It also risks the steady danger that the husband will find his office associates understand him better than his family. The surprised widow who meets at her husband's funeral for the first time many people who found their lives touched in important ways by her husband, realizes how little she knew the man to whom she was married.

"Spouse phobia." In a little volume on psychotherapy written over a decade ago three authors working together chose as their illustrative case a problem in the relation between a husband and a wife which they called "spouse phobia." (6) The irrational, anxiety-tinged avoidance of the marital partner was the situation in their case illustration. They chose this particular case because of their conviction about its prevalence as a phenomenon in marriage today. It may seem surprising that people freely choosing to be partners for life should find avoidance of that partner cropping up inside the marriage. But the truth is that marriage as an experience of growing intimacy is not an automatic result of a wedding ceremony or a shared bed.

Romantic illusions hover around the institution of marriage. Magical changes are expected because the prince charming and the lovely princess pledge their troth to each other. True inner freedom from constriction in affective expression has little to do with ceremonies and surface appearances. The individual who has negative avoidances of the sexual aspects of life conditioned from early childhood will find that these reactive conditionings go right on operating in the years of marriage. Juvenile utilizations of the sexual partnership for conquest will pale when the warfare is over and the opponent becomes a partner. Marriage can become the moment of transition from attraction to avoidance.

In a society which seems to be as sexually emancipated as America today appears, it might be suspected that "spouse phobia" is on the wane. Open talk about sex and culture-wide preoccupation with sex hardly suggest that we are as "emancipated" in the sexual sphere as we tend to think. Even radically changing premarital and extramarital sexual behavior is not a clue to sexual emancipation. Rather the very signs of increasing sexual freedom tend to suggest increasing bondage to sexuality as the exclusive meaning of the male-female relation. What is missing in the encounter with sexuality in our society is the effective integration of intimacy needs between two people and their needs for physical sexual expression.

Intimacy as the sustained warmth and caring of two people for each other is distinguishable from sexuality. Interpersonal maturity as Harry Stack Sullivan defined it requires the convergence of the person who is the object of intimacy needs and the person who is the object of sexual needs. (12) When the objects of these two needs diverge, then the one who is the object of sexual passions becomes a thing rather than a person. When intimacy needs are extracted into some pure essence then we have the tender care for an infant but not an adult heterosexual relationship. Much of the turbulence and anguish of adolescence revolves around the difficulty which the emerging adult in our society has in effecting the integration of these two great need systems. They can be in opposition and much of our society places them in opposition, Freud and Kinsey notwithstanding. During long stretches of childhood these two systems are well compartmentalized. Marriage is too often a continuation of the antagonism or the compartmentalization of these two need systems.

The study of *Plainville, USA* by James West (8) was subjected to psychoanalytic scrutiny by Abraham Kardiner. He was startled by a community which handled engagement and marriage with secrecy because of its potential sexual embarrassment and shame. In the mating itself, he observed:

. . . hidden constellations come to the fore. Difficulties may arise in connection with the tender relations to the mate, or with the sensual relations. In the first instance various degrees of anxiety and mistrust may pervade the relationship. In the sensual field a large number of potency disturbance may be precipitated. . . . In the case of the female the sexual situation is about the same. In Plainville frigidity is likely to be the norm.[2]

If the factors present in Plainville, U.S.A. are in some degree a part of the American, then the typical adult in our society shelters embarrassment and uncertainty about his own sexuality. Social psychologists have effectively made this point. They forcefully declare the white adult is preoccupied with sex and has a bad conscience about it. The white American's stereotype of the Negro as oversexed is a projection. The white American projects upon the socially disapproved Negro his own unacceptable desires regarding sexuality. Then he feels justified in disapproval of the Negro while at the same time he conceals from himself his own unseemly sexual appetites. (11)

A startling testimony to "spouse phobia" is found in the report of "Wife Swapping" systematized by classified ads through a mimeographed magazine emanating from Pacifica, California. A San Francisco news couple who interviewed, unawares, countless of the couples by placing ads in this magazine reported the frequent justification for this cheating in concert was that it "saved our marriage."[3] The surprising finding beyond this one was the outward ordinariness of the couples interviewed by the reporters. The bizarreness of the solution to unhappy sexual adjustment in their marriages resorted to by the couples interviewed may well be the only extraordinary aspect of their lives. That there is boredom, emptiness, disinterest in the marriage and avoidance of the marital partner, may be more ordinary than we yet recognize in our society.

The more typical solution acted upon when the romantic glow of courtship and honeymoon fades is suggested in the frank discussion a housewife wrote to one research worker as follows:

What is it like to be married to a person you don't love, and who cannot make himself feel love for you? First, you have to pretend, and this requires you to be constantly on guard. For a few years you

---

[2] Abraham Kardiner, *The Psychological Frontiers of Society* (New York: Columbia University Press, 1945), pp. 363–364.

[3] Paul and Emily Avery, "Some Notes on 'Wife Swapping'" reprinted in Henry A. Grunwald, Editor, *Sex in America* (New York: Bantam Books, Inc., 1964), pp. 248–254.

hope that one day you'll wake up and find you've fallen in love with your husband; but slowly you realize that although there are brief moments of physical passion, there will never come a union of souls. The empty place in your heart grows, and for no tangible reason you feel guilty. I sometimes think that being unfaithful would not fill me with such remorse as the knowledge that I am not, and never will be, in love with my husband. We tried togetherness, but the strain was too great; now we gracefully find reasons to be apart, in our separate clubs and activities. We never talk about it.[4]

Gracefully finding "reasons to be apart" is the dilemma of many marriages. And the concluding prescription may also be the source of the illness, "we never talk about it."

Training in intimacy. The quiet desperation and drifting apart which comes to many couples can be counteracted by offering to married couples the opportunity to learn how to talk to each other. The intimacy crisis is not going to be overcome by a change in the separation of work and home in our society. Nor is the isolated, highly mobile conjugal family apt to cease to be normative. But rather than presume there is nothing to do but watch the strains of intimacy being placed upon the small circle of the immediate family, we can take steps to widen the circle of a caring fellowship.

The church is the place where the caring of persons for others as persons may be sponsored. The small group is the genius of pastoral care here. The formation of the Couples Concern Groups is one way in which the *koinonia* we have in Christ may be expressed. It offers contemporary marriages a training ground in the meaning of intimacy. It is a place to learn how to talk to others about things which matter deeply in Christian life and witness. It is a place wherein such serious talk is not divided between the sexes. It is a place where learning to speak in meaningful personal terms within a small mixed company turns out to be a rehearsal for couples to carry on such conversation with each other.

The problem is not how to ignite romantic glows in some mystical, emotive form. The problem is how to help two people take each other seriously as persons. It is the problem of helping two people to talk to each other about the little and the large matters of their

---

[4] From *Her Infinite Variety* by Morton M. Hunt. Reprinted by permission of Harper & Row, Publishers.

lives before the crisis state when neither spouse can nor will communicate. Such a contribution is the one which the Couples Christian Concern Group can make to people who, however well educated, have not been educated in our society on how to live the years past the marriage ceremony and honeymoon.

The Crisis of Parenthood

Untrained parents. The splitting off of the young couple at the moment of marriage from the families in which each was reared into their own family unit seems to be quite workable at first. Children come a little later. The Fairchild and Wynn study found that the sociologists talk about the crisis of marriage and mislead many into thinking the crisis which divorce statistics signal occurred at the moment of marriage. Instead they found that married persons actually report less strain and difficulty in the initial adjustment to each other than expected. What they did report, however, was the degree of unpreparedness felt by married couples for assuming the role of parents. Parents interviewed in the Fairchild and Wynn study said, "It is parenthood, not marriage, that requires the greater step into maturity."[5]

At this juncture we can see another consequence of the isolated, conjugal family in a highly mobile society. The kind of wisdom which one generation gains in rearing a family is not available to the next. The new marriage starts a new family. Parents of both families of orientation are left behind. When children come along the wisdom of experienced parents is out of reach or rejected out of hand. Few periods in family life are counted more trying than the days or weeks when a grandparent comes to help out the new mother and father. Even if the ways of a grandparent are wise, they are still taken as an intrusion into an arena of sacred right belonging to the new parents. The tremendous reliance upon Dr. Spock's book of common sense for the mothers of infants is testimony to the almost total rejection of the same kind of advice were it to be received from a grandparent of the child. A paperback book with a scientific *imprimatur* is a far preferable source of knowledge for the "modern" mother. (17) The fact of the matter is that young people receive

---

[5] Roy W. Fairchild, and John C. Wynn, *Families in the Church*, New York: Association Press, 1961, p. 140.

very little or no training at all in the most important human role which is thrust upon them. A romantic blindspot surrounds parent-hood which is fully as serious as the one which attends marriage. Just because two people can procreate a third human being it is assumed that they can attend to its wants and needs adequately. Occasionally one or the other parent has had a course in Family Life or Child Development. Rarely have they studied together the way to meet the new role as parent.

There is an awareness of this problem on the part of many pastors which has led to forming classes for parents of newly baptized children. This is a natural point in the life of the church where as pastors we can help parents. But even so, the problem of being un-trained to be a parent continues throughout the whole stretch of years from infancy to maturity. The evidence of this is the request of parents for help from the church at each successive stage of development beyond infancy. The point of greatest anxiety in the minds of parents is the period of years immediately ahead of their oldest child. Here is the unknown. Once they have lived through this zone with one child it is never quite so threatening again. Younger siblings are the inheritors of the parental wisdom gained with the first child. Unfortunately we cannot throw first-borns away when they have completed training an adult couple how to be more relaxed and accomplished parents. The imperative is to provide some way of helping the parents to meet with adequacy the problems of each successive stage of child and youth development.

Confusion over discipline. The point of great uncertainty for parents is what to do in balancing *control with love*. If each of these factors is taken as a necessary ingredient of the parent-child rela-tion, then some of the combinations can be diagrammed as in Figure 1. When either too much or too little of one dimension is combined with too much or too little of the other dimension, the results are regularly unfortunate. What this diagram shows is the combining of love and control which is required of parents.

As new psychological wisdom came from psychoanalytic circles it had pendulum effects upon parentage during the last two gener-ations. By the early 1930's there were all manner of books being written to counteract strictness in discipline with pleas for permis-siveness so as to reduce the fierceness of "super-ego" assault upon

FIGURE 1:   Possible Parent-Child Relationships

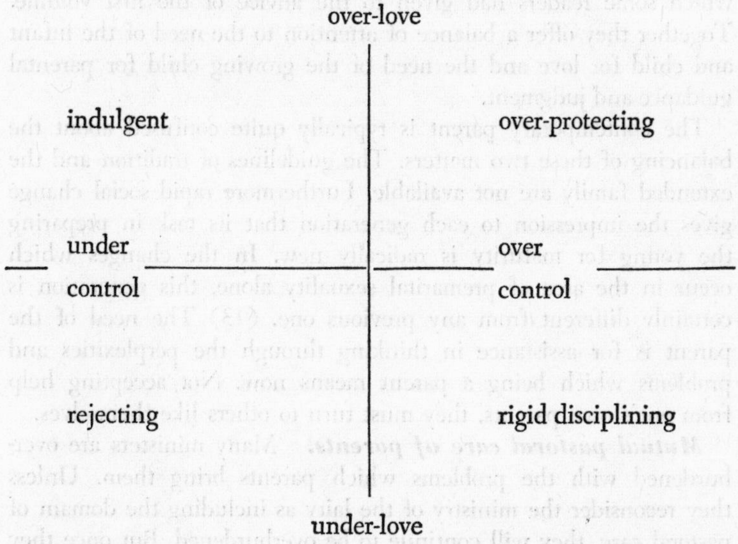

over-love

indulgent   over-protecting

under   over

control   control

rejecting   rigid disciplining

under-love

the "ego." Parents who joined the *avant-garde* of permissiveness discovered they were spawning results more demonic than that displaced. Psychological writers and pediatricians like Dr. Spock have tried to bring a "common sense" equilibrium to discipline and affection during the last two decades.

One of the problems in relating love and discipline is the fact that the balance between the two changes with the emerging capacity for independent action and expression of the growing child. Two very helpful books for parents while representing in part the pendulum swing of advice from psychological writers actually differ greatly in their stress upon love and permissiveness because of the change of focus from infancy to childhood. Margaret Ribble's *The Rights of Infants* (19) laid strong emphasis upon the need of the infant for unconditional love because she was writing about early infancy. In her sequel volume, *The Personality of the Young Child*, (20) Margaret Ribble stresses the parent's role in guidance and setting limits to behavior. The difference in her advice has to do with the changing needs of the child. But part of the necessity for writing the second volume was the mistaken overgeneralization which some readers had given to the advice of the first volume. Together they offer a balance of attention to the need of the infant and child for love and the need of the growing child for parental guidance and judgment.

The contemporary parent is typically quite confused about the balancing of these two matters. The guidelines of tradition and the extended family are not available. Furthermore rapid social change gives the impression to each generation that its task in preparing the young for maturity is radically new. In the changes which occur in the area of premarital sexuality alone, this generation is certainly different from any previous one. (13) The need of the parent is for assistance in thinking through the perplexities and problems which being a parent means now. Not accepting help from one's own parents, they must turn to others like themselves.

Mutual pastoral care of parents. Many ministers are overburdened with the problems which parents bring them. Unless they reconsider the ministry of the laity as including the domain of pastoral care, they will continue to be overburdened. But once they take seriously the capacity of ordinary people to "bear one another's burdens" they will find that the ministry of the laity gains one important expression in the *koinonia* group. It is not that parents need courses for each stage of parentage, but that the church should be so organized as to provide a caring fellowship throughout the journey of life so that whenever couples face problems they may be helped readily and naturally. The Couples Christian Concern Groups are a way of organizing the life of parish parents in small groups so that they may provide the ministry of mutual care for each other.

We have tended to think about pastoral care and counseling as though it were the exclusive prerogative of the set-apart ministry. Part of the reason for this is the great interest pastors themselves have shown in the role of being a counselor. It gives them some relief from the problem of the role maceration and it has appeared to offer a more commanding identity in a clinically attuned age. But the essential ingredients of a helping relationship are not peculiarly clinical nor narrowly pastoral. As the aspects of a helping relation are set forth by Carl Rogers we find three significant elements:

(1) *Congruence in the helping person.*

By this I mean that whatever feeling or attitude I am experiencing would be matched by my awareness of that attitude. When this is true, then I am a unified or integrated person in that moment, and hence I can *be* whatever I deeply *am*. This is a reality which I find others experience as dependable.[6]

This also means to be "transparently real."

If I can form a helping relationship to myself—if I can be sensitively aware of and acceptant toward my own feelings—then the likelihood is great that I can form a helping relationship toward another.[7]

(2) *Caring*

Can I let myself experience positive attitudes toward this other person—attitudes of warmth, liking, interest, respect? . . . It is a real achievement when we can learn, even in certain relationships or at certain times in those relationships, that it is safe to care, that it is safe to relate to the other as a person for whom we have positive feelings.[8]

(3) *Empathic openness to another.*

Can I let myself enter fully into the world of his feelings and personal meanings and see these as he does?[9]

It is important to note that none of these elements of a helping relationship is precisely embodied in any given procedure of counseling. These significant elements have to do with the attitudes and the values of one person relative to another. A helping relationship, even one offered by a trained counselor, is constituted in its essence by ingredients which are very elemental even if not obvious. The knowledge of psychodynamics, personality theory and psychopathology are not the clues to what is critically central in the therapeutic equation. Such equipment makes technical experts but not necessarily able therapists. The clues to what is really therapeutic as

---

[6] Carl R. Rogers, *On Becoming a Person* (Boston: Houghton Mifflin Company, 1961), p. 51.

[7] *Ibid.*, p. 51.

[8] *Ibid.*, p. 52.

[9] *Ibid.*, p. 53.

offered by Rogers are very much of a piece with what the Christian faith has understood as its ethic of love.

The work of Christian love belongs to every disciple of Christ. It is not enjoined upon pastors alone. What each Christian needs is an occasion for exercising the potentials of caring for the life of another which have been given to him. Too often the sole expectation of pastors with regard to their parishioners is faithful attendance at services of worship. The passivity of the participation even in "congregational" forms of worship is such as to invite the most feminine qualities of the human community to the fore. At the very point where we might expect to challenge the more robust elements of the community by specifying a Christian discipline for members we tend to lose conviction and worry about expecting too much of our people. Yet the discipline of participation in a small group wherein the exercise of the capacity for Christian caring takes place has appeal to men as well as women. Wherever this kind of discipline has been tried, leaders speak of "renewal" of the life of the church in glowing terms. (28, 29, 30, 31, 32) As the Johannine writer suggests, "doing the truth" unfolds the fellowship Christians have with each other. (I John ll:6, 7)

The formation of a Couples Christian Concern Group extends the ministry of the laymen to each other in mutual caring and burden bearing. It is a discipline which gives exercise to the love of neighbor rather than mere lip service. It is a natural constitution of the life of the congregation through which contemporary parents may minister to each other as parents.

The Crisis of Purpose

The pruning of the family. Many large social purposes which now lie outside the family once had their location within the family. Economic productivity belonged to the family of colonial times. The goods and requirements of family survival were largely the responsibility of the collaborative industry of all family members. The more members the more mouths to feed, but also the more hands to share in the support of the family. The factory system in the first industrial revolution changed all this for town families. Now the mechanization of the farm is virtually eliminating the "family" farm. The size and cohesion of the family is not a significant factor in the economic development of our society the way it was at one time. The family has an economic role in assuring continued support of its members, but at all points where the family fails to fulfill this role, social welfare agencies step in. The chronically unemployed are viewed as a responsibility of the society at large, hence the war on poverty of President Johnson. The mentally incapacitated are the responsibility of the state, hence the state and national programs of care for the mentally ill and mentally retarded. The physically handicapped are assisted by state programs of rehabilitation. The deserted mother and child receives aid for dependent children. The elderly are on social security. Every form of economic dependency which arises within the family is now considered a collective responsibility of the larger society. Assistance at times of catastrophic hospitalization is just the most recent of these claims to be advanced. The family itself is not considered the unit of economic survival in the contemporary world.

The family as the place of religious education is no longer of primary significance. The assumption that children should be processed through church schools on a grade escalator paralleling the public school is now quite universal. A considerable share of the more than one billion dollars a year spent on new church building is going to provide church facilities for Christian education. An indication of the complete surrender of religious nurture to those outside the family was seen in the national resistance to the 1962 Supreme Court Regents' Prayer decision. Excluding the teaching of prayer from the province of the public school was reacted to by many as an attack upon religion. The absence of any attempt on the part of parents to be the religious educators of their children in matters of prayer is what makes the violence of such a reaction somewhat intelligible.

The use of leisure is not even a responsibility of the family. Except for the family vacation which still exists, the use of leisure is looked after by the mass communication industry and the recreation industry. The purchase of the New York Yankees by Columbia Broadcasting System in 1964 was jauntily justified by the common interest of television and spectator sports in supplying viewers with endless hours of entertainment.

One by one the functions of the family have been pruned away leaving only procreation, the early socialization of the child and the continuing nurture in intimacy as the distinctive purposes of the family. These would be purposes of significant spiritual value were the awareness of the meaning of persons grounded in the Christian faith. But when the awareness of the meaning of persons is grounded only in democratic humanism and psychological insight, then even the purpose remaining in the family domain seems weak and mutable. Thus the pruning of various social functions from the family tends to leave the contemporary family without a real, viable purpose. That God calls human persons into being in and through the family in order that they might through Christ become sons of the Father which is God sounds all right. However, not many families see themselves aligned to such a high purpose. To most the pruning of family functions down to its present level has been to strip the organism of its vital structures.

The emptiness of affluence. The ethos of the wider culture affects the family mightily. Americans have been enjoying a sustained economic development which has brought increasing numbers and an increasing percentage of the people into the economic well-being of middle class life. To be sure the record is not that of the "Great Society" yet. What were pockets of poverty have enlarged into residual strongholds requiring warfare to overcome them. The racial blindness of the affluent society has been massive. But overall the picture is still one of greater prosperity for a greater portion of the people of a society than ever before achieved in human history.

For many people it is not until the dream of utopia as a two-car existence in a well-landscaped suburban development has been achieved that they come to realize the awesome externality of these goals. The complacent quietude of the 1950's led to the call for a vision of our national purpose. For a time in the 1960's it looked as though our national purpose were to be found in youthfulness and its future, then in our common mourning. Now it seems we shall return to the old depression-tested purposes of stamping out residual poverty, unemployment, educational deprivation and economic hardship without regard for race.

We seem as a nation to be imprisoned by the economic virtues of the affluent society. The ethos of economic success and material well-being saturates the air we breathe so heavily that even in the inner-city where the reality of economic affluence is least present the air still is filled with its desires. We are one nation in our striving after economic well-being. What is missing is a transcending claim upon us beyond the economic one. Are we to strive toward the great society of economic success so that we can be a more human community of the people of God? Is there any goal beyond the material and economic one which the nation-state can raise for itself in a sophisticated post-Christendom culture?

Our questions of purpose and destiny are raised with regard to the nation as a whole because that is the wider context which affects the family. The religious purpose of the pilgrim family grew out of the purpose of the pilgrim community. Similarly the contemporary emptiness of the family in its sense of high destiny before God reflects a measure of the larger national vacuity of purpose.

Nurture for mission. The family's role as the place of nurturance of the young person is insufficient purpose for the Christian family. Nurture for what? Nurture for nurture's sake does not indicate that a Christian's style of life also is at stake. Nurturance suggests only self-development which may be indistinguishable from psychological maturity. The answer to the crisis of purpose which confronts family life today is not to be found in the use of the small group for parent couples as though the small group principle were the secret of success.

Small group life in the churches as a form of renewal has received a scathing attack at the hands of one writer:

> As far as group dynamics is concerned, the small group is close to being a 'good' group . . . Group members are loyal to the group and find satisfaction in the group activities. . . . Some groups are not tyrannical; they are vicious. For this reason we should see that group dynamics and the small groups multiplying like hamsters in the church today have little to do with each other. The small group is closer to traditional Protestant piety than it is to Kurt Lewin, and thus closer to the standard situation than to the breakaway group.[10]

---

[10] John R. Fry, *A Hard Look at Adult Christian Education* (Philadelphia: The Westminster Press, 1961), pp. 27–28.

What John R. Fry rightly attacks here is the suggestion of self-sufficient purpose adhering to the small group simply because it is a small group in the church.

A similar discovery was made by the Church of Our Saviour in Washington, D.C., which utilized membership in a small group as one of the disciplines for members from the very beginning. The consultative help of Elton Trueblood had stressed the value of the small group as a form of sharing in the Christian life. But in the mid-1950's the leadership of the congregation became convinced that the small group life was a nurturing fellowship all right, but that it was not issuing in Christian witness. Rather than abandon the value of the small group idea, they reformed the membership in new groups and labeled all the groups as "Mission" groups. In these reformed small groups, nurture as mutual caring and sustaining of each other continued to be important. But the reason for being was not nurture alone. The reason for being extended out into the world and into the life of Christian witness and service in the world. Out of the groups emerged three new forms of congregational structure for being the church in the world: Dayspring, the camp and retreat area in the country; Retreat House, a pastoral counseling residential center at Dayspring; and The Potter's House, the pioneer of the Christian coffee houses.[11]

While we are noting that nurture without mission can be introversive, it is important to say the reverse. The small Christian group existing for mission beyond itself without attention to the values of mutual caring which we are calling nurture gives false testimony to the Christian evangel. The church in mission to the world should be subject to the observation of the outsider, "See how they love one another."

For the church to be a servant church in mission to the world, it is necessary that it take its purpose for being in both a faith and a work which reach beyond introversive pleasures. But it is also

---

[11] Elizabeth O'Conner, *The Call to Commitment* (New York: Harper & Row, Pubilshers, 1962). Some of the background regarding the change-over in the structuring of small group life in the Church of Our Saviour came from personal conversation with Elizabeth O'Conner in 1961. The spread of coffee houses under Christian auspices has become a truly phenomenal event. Over 100 such places are now operating under church auspices in the United States.

necessary that Christians receive adequate strengthening from each other so that they may turn outward to the needs of the world knowing themselves to be different as Christians. Nurture groups for the sake of nurture cannot acquit the Christian's reason for being in fellowship with other Christians. But mission to the world by the lay apostolate requires strengthened faith and life in each Christian.

The Couples Christian Concern Group is one means of restructuring the life of the congregation so that the church may free itself from the bonds of traditional organizational self-serving and introversiveness. It is a means of helping the church find its purpose in being a church in mission to the world. It is a means of regaining the world-directed side of the church's and of the individual Christian's ministry. It is a means also of helping the family to see its purpose is to be found in the mission of the church to the world. At one and the same time the Couples Christian Concern Group addresses itself to the crisis of purpose in the contemporary family and culture and the crisis of introversion and organizational self-serving which afflicts the churches. It is the family which sends a missioner to the world each day in the person of its breadwinner.

The address of the Couples Christian Concern Group to the mission of the Christian as witness and service in the world arises by reason of the fact that it takes the work of each partner as his place of *Christian* vocation. It is around this focus of being called to serve as a Christian through one's daily vocation that the "concerns" arise. The group permits fellow Christians to speak to the quandaries and predicaments of Christian service in one's given work. To be sure, one of the partners finds her place of Christian vocation in the home and the local community: hence the family and parental focus of many of the concerns which she raises. But the other partner is the family's missionary agent to the places of decision and power affecting the life of the total community today. What he does at such points of decision determine whether or not there is a lay apostolate to the world. There is a lively issue of the "worldly service" of the Christian and the "secular relevance of the gospel" raised by the questions and concerns of the husband and father as he seeks to be a Christian in his place of daily work.

Some may object that this deals only with the Christian as an individual and not with the Christian witness as a corporate strategy for meeting and serving the world's needs. Or it may be objected that this form of equipping the Christian for being in mission to the world may not sufficiently challenge what needs to be challenged in the structures of contemporary urban alienation, segregation and dehumanization. These objections have some legitimacy and should caution us against assuming that the whole of the purpose of the Christian colony in the world is fulfilled through the apostolate of the laity in daily vocations.

The multiple crises which place the family under stress today can be spoken to by a new form of pastoral care. The Couples Christian Concern Group is pastoral care meeting crises between marital partners, with parents in distress over their responsibilities, and in the church's and the Christian's call to servanthood under a servant Christ.

CHAPTER TWO

CONGREGATIONAL CARE

In the previous chapter we have seen the issues and needs in marriage and family today which may be helped by Couples Christians Concern Groups. We have already indicated that the small caring fellowship is a potential form of pastoral care. It is a form which has not been utilized as fully as it should. To see the meaning of the small caring group as pastoral care we shall locate it first in relation to the total work of the pastor.

Forms of Pastoral Care

Ordinary pastoral care. The normal avenue of pastoral care to the individual and to the family is the communication of the Gospel of Jesus Christ. It is a message of the reconciliation which God has accomplished for sinful men in the life, death and resurrection of Jesus Christ. This message is open ended. The work of God for our salvation was accomplished once for all in Jesus Christ. Yet the work of Jesus Christ continues through the Holy Spirit in the work of reconciliation which God has called us to share. Paul's words to the Corinthians guide us here:

> Therefore, if any one is in Christ, he is a new creation; the old has passed away, behold the new has come. All this is from God, who through Christ reconciled us to himself and gave us the ministry of reconciliation; that is, God was in Christ reconciling the world to himself, not counting their trespasses against them, and entrusting to us the message of reconciliation. So we are ambassadors for Christ, God making his appeal through us. (II Corinthians 5:17–20; RSV)

The message of God's reconciliation also calls us into the ministry of reconciliation, the continuing of God's appeal through Christian disciples. The redemption which God accomplished in Jesus Christ is our message. The redemptive work which God continues to effect through Jesus Christ is a ministry into which we too are called. Both the message and the ministry of reconciliation are important.

The message of reconciliation between sinful men and God points to the great "care" of God for men. The celebration of Jesus Christ as God's own testimony of his caring is pastoral care in the broadest sense. Hence the preaching of God's Word, celebration of the Eucharist, study and teaching of the Word are all ways in which God's caring is extended through ordinary pastoral work. It is unfortunate that pastoral care has come to be defined so narrowly in terms of the specialized ministry of counseling that its connection with the message of reconciliation has been tenuous. We can correct this by remembering that the ministry of reconciliation of which we are to be agents[1] is integrally bound up with the message of reconciliation.

Extraordinary pastoral care.   Another way of reminding ourselves of the intimate relation between the message and the ministry of reconciliation is to adopt a distinction put forth by Wilhelm Löhe,[2] a German pastor and teacher of the 19th century. The more narrow functions of pastoral care with individuals were specified by him as extraordinary forms of pastoral care. A long tradition within the church has held that this individual pastoral work is the typical meaning of pastoral care.[3] It is this tradition focused upon *what the pastor does* which has provided the background for the functional turn of pastoral care in the modern American scene. The difference between the functionalism of pastoral care today and that which previous history held is simply the psychological orientation of the moderns.

---

[1] See Arnold Come's book, *Agents of Reconciliation* (Philadelphia: The Westminster Press, 1960) for a helpful understanding of the relation between that which God has accomplished in Jesus Christ and the ministry to which every Christian is called.

[2] Wilhelm Löhe's understanding of pastoral care embraced this broad understanding of all ways in which the Gospel of God's forgiveness toward sinners is proclaimed in church life. Cf. Wilhelm Löhe, *Gesammelte Werke* (Neuendettelsau: Freimundsverlag, 1951–1962).

[3] Cf. John T. McNeill, *A History of the Cure of Souls* (New York: Harper & Row, Publishers, 1951).

Eduard Thurneysen (71) has offered a great corrective to the functional bias of individual pastoral care by his insistence that the message of God's forgiveness for sinners is central both to preaching and to pastoral conversation. One way in which he does this is to draw upon Calvin's teaching regarding the marks of the church. The true nature of the church as presented by Calvin includes church discipline. Thurneysen views church discipline as the logical basis for individual pastoral care. Hence when Calvin sees the church as existing where Word, Sacrament and discipline are provided, Thurneysen is able to see the church where Word, Sacrament and individual pastoral care are offered. The integral relation of pastoral care to individuals and pastoral care through word and sacrament to the whole congregation is based upon their common standing in the essence of the church.

A parallel argument for the unity of the message and the ministry in pastoral care is found in Thurneysen's insistence that the purpose of both is proclamation of the Word of God. Thurneysen's attempt to find the unity of general and special pastoral work in this direction becomes most strained. He understands and stresses the importance of listening in individual pastoral care:

. . . one must be prepared in the pastoral conversation as nowhere else to be a listener—a patient, concentrated, attentive, alert, and understanding listener and nothing else. Everything depends on our ability to listen, our desire to listen and our urge to listen, totally involved, for the sake of the Word that now intends to go forth to the man unfolding his situation to us.[4]

It is clear that Thurneysen is recommending functions other than proclamatory ones when he speaks of the pastor's role in the pastoral conversation. Even though listening is for the sake of the Word which is to go forth, it is quite a stretch of language to hold the concept of proclamation to cover both patient listening and the offering of the Word in its individual relevance.

We prefer a different choice of language to accomplish the same goals Thurneysen has, namely the recognition that individual pastoral care is grounded in Christology fully as much as ordinary

---

[4] Eduard Thurneysen, *A Theology of Pastoral Care* (Richmond: John Knox Press, 1962), pp. 127–128.

pastoral care through preaching the Word and administering the sacraments. In choosing to speak of God's reconciliation in Christ we refer both to a message and to a ministry. In ordinary pastoral care we stress the message of God's reconciliation. In extraordinary pastoral care we stress the ministry of reconciliation to which God has called us. Neither the message nor the ministry exhausts the richness of the meaning of the reconciliation which God has accomplished and continues to accomplish in Jesus Christ.

To see the essential Christological unity of ordinary and extraordinary pastoral care is important. However to focus upon this unity as Thurneysen does in terms of the proclamatory is also to blind ourselves to another vital form of pastoral care. The Corinthian passage quoted which has given us the concept of reconciliation by which to see the unity of "ordinary" and of individualized forms of pastoral care, also lifts to our awareness this additional aspect of pastoral care. This is the fact that the ministry of reconciliation belongs to every Christian. Pastoral care as a form of the proclamation of the Word can easily be seen as the special province of the ordained ministry with preaching the Word and administering the sacraments. But pastoral care seen as the message and ministry of reconciliation cannot be so restricted.

Congregational care.   Pastoral care as the message and ministry of reconciliation belongs to the gathered church and to the scattered church. Every Christian is to be an agent of reconciliation. This ministry has been given to all. Because pastoral care in both its ordinary concern with the message of reconciliation and in its extraordinary concern with the ministry of reconciliation to individuals has been so identified with the care of souls which pastors exercise, we choose to speak of the lay ministry in pastoral care as *congregational care.*

When we consider *congregational care* as a third form of pastoral care we become involved in questions about the structure of congregational life. Unless the life of the gathered community of believers provides opportunity for real meeting and mutual knowing, there can be only the most fragmentary caring.

Congregational care cannot be exercised in gathering for public worship. The center of worship is God's Word and our response in praise, prayer and understanding. It is not an occasion for exchange between persons. But neither can *congregational care* be provided by the usual organizational life of the churches. The groups within the church which suggest the possibility of personal exchange actually devote immense energies to programs and to rounding up attendance for them. The age-sex societies in the church are examples of organizational life which usually promote nothing quite so well as their own organization: the Women's Group, the Men's Group, the Couples Group and the Youth Group.

The chief hazards of these normal congregational groupings are threefold. For one thing they have Christian fellowship as an end. This is a vague and yet "right" sounding goal. But Christian fellowship is a by-product rather than the goal of Christian life together. Christian fellowship is not just fellowship. It is not some form of holy chumminess. It is depth of caring which comes to those who are joined to others because of being joined to Christ first. It is fellowship experienced by those who are together in Christ.

The second hazard of our age-sex organizational life is its "officer complex." The election of a few to be responsible does a number of things to any group. It limits to a few the feeling of responsibility for the group. It extends to the few the rewards of a fuller relationship with each other as a by-product of the mutual effort to organize the group for others. It creates systems of organizational motivation by which the officers seek to justify themselves. Thus they plan programs bound to secure the largest turnout and so prove their creative leadership by counting heads. The quality of what is done through its conformity to the mind of Christ is difficult to measure and has little credit value in the world of organizational success anyway. Thus the groups take on an immense amount of their character not as ways of upbuilding the life of a Christian congregation but as devices for building up the leadership image of a few people.

The third hazard of the age-sex groupings in the church is their dependence upon the occasional appearance of someone with organizational talents in order to look alive. The reason why the appearance is occasional is because the rigors of wheel turning devour so much time and energy that the sustained commitment of anyone is precluded. Thus the typical church organization is a monster on the prowl. It is an organization which demands and devours leadership. It does so in ways which have more to do with its own numerical livelihood than the liveliness of the gospel.

If the ministry of the laity in pastoral care is to be exercised in *congregational care,* new forms of structuring the life of the congregation are required. The small group structured in terms of a meaningful discipline is an answer which has emerged in countless places in our time. By limiting the size of each group to ten or twelve persons we find that knowledge of other persons is possible at a more than superficial level. Leadership by a few is no longer crucial. The purpose for being does not get ground to dust in the machinery of keeping the organization alive. Small groups can come into existence and pass into oblivion with few hurt egos. The life of the group is more easily kept responsive to its intrinsic reason for being. When that intrinsic purpose no longer is generative or compelling, change is possible without upheaval.

Within the small group the laity have the opportunity to exercise their ministry of pastoral care. One cannot care for five hundred people at once, nor even thirty-five. But one can come to know ten or twelve people with sufficient fulness to bear each as a person in his own right. *Congregational care* means many small units of a congregation entered upon a discipline of life together. It is the little church within the church (*ecclesiola in ecclesia*). But it is not the little church of the pious few. It is a little church as a representative sample of the larger gathering. It is necessary that it be small so that caring rather than organizational perpetuation comes to the fore.

Pastoral oversight of congregational care. A fourth form of pastoral care is required as a consequence of identifying the third form as the ministry of the laity, or the mutual ministry, in pastoral care. This is the work of fostering and overseeing *congregational care* in small groups. If the ministry of the laity includes care for others as persons, then the ordained ministry given "for the equipment of the saints, for the work of ministry, for building up the body of Christ," (Ephesians 4:12) is an organizing ministry. In the area of pastoral care it is the ministry which provides the opportunity for the ministry of the laity.

Initiating and overseeing a group so that it will be a group concerned with persons, so that it will be a group in which pastoral care is mutually extended, requires organizing. We have indicated already that we are talking about new structures of congregational life. We are also in need of new understandings of the contribution of the ordained minister. Just as the new accent upon the ministry of the laity has stressed that the ordained minister is not the chief Christian in the congregation, so also must we underscore that the ordained minister is not to think of himself as the chief member of the group.

In the small group the resources of leadership are drawn from within the group. To facilitate the emergence of leadership functions in others the minister steps back from his customary leadership role in the congregation. In the small group he stands *with* the members of his flock and *behind* them. To help a group find and develop its own leadership potentials the pastor makes three contributions:

(1) he convenes the group initially;
(2) he sets a trial pattern for its work together;
(3) and he provides resources for the group to evaluate the life of the group.

He does not have to be the source of the thinking of the group, nor does he have to draw conclusions and implications for group members. When the pattern for the group's work together has been set effectively the members themselves will think things through and make contributions to each other of care, interest and understanding which will exceed his resources however considerable they may be.

The clear implication of the small group as a means of *congregational care* is that the pastor need not be, as indeed he cannot be, present in each group every time it meets. His work becomes one of oversight to the life of many groups. In so far as we are talking about groups which have pastoral care or the nurture of persons as one aspect of their being, then the pastor is truly a pastor to pastors. He is a bishop, overseeing the pastoral work of many.

This schematic look at the forms of pastoral care relates all pastoral care to the gospel as the message of God's reconciling work in Jesus Christ; it identifies the pastor's work with individuals as an expression of the ministry of reconciliation; it helps us see that the ministry of reconciliation belongs to every member—a ministry we have specified as *congregational care* to emphasize that it is supplemental to the pastor's agency; and by this scheme we see another responsibility of the pastor—organizing and overseeing a congregation so that the laity may fulfill its work of ministry to persons. This outline gives us an adequate perspective from which to consider one way in which *congregational care* may be facilitated. We readily acknowledge the experience of many others in which *congregational care* in small groups has come into existence through Bible study, evangelistic missions, adult study and prayer groups. Our report is of small groups as organized in the Glenview, Illinois, Community Church during the period of the "Team Ministry"[5] and which have continued subsequently.

The Couples Christian Concern Group

The background.   The beginning use of the Couples Group as a form of pastoral care was somewhat accidental. In conjunction with the operation of a church nursery school in the Glenview Community Church during the late 1940's, Phoebe Anderson as the director of that school and her minister-husband, Philip Anderson, gathered the parents of the nursery children in an evening group. They were convinced that any problems which the parents were having with the children were not because there was some problem in the children. Rather they assumed that any problem in the parent-child relation was a reflection of some parental conflict. The Andersons saw that their task was not to superimpose the Gesell manual on the child. It was instead the task of illuminating for the parents the tensions, pressures and conflicts inside themselves and in their behavior toward the children, to which the children were resonating. To accomplish this purpose they used devices of role-playing and other techniques which the group dynamics people were discovering. The parent who joined the group for the purpose of understanding the nursery-age child dis-

---

[5] See the March, 1963 issue of *Pastoral Psychology* on "The Ministry as a Team." The report of the Glenview Community Church is found in the article by Robert A. Edgar, "A Ten Year Experiment," Vol. 14, No. 132, pp. 19–24.

covered he was learning something about himself. The completion of the stated series of meetings did not complete the task which the parents now saw. It only awakened for them the fact that they had a work of being persons to others as a way of Christian growth which they themselves needed to pursue.

Under the skillful hand of the initiator of Glenview's team ministry, Robert A. Edgar, the applicability of this small parents group idea to other couples as a means whereby they could grow in Christian caring and deepening understanding of their own impediments to Christian love was sensed and seized.[6] The focus upon changes in themselves as persons was widened by adopting the Friends' term "concern." The subject matter for the discussion was now not limited to the parent-child relation. A "concern" tends to arise at the point where one is fully engaged with life. A Christian concern is the issue of the relevance of the Gospel at the point where one meets the problematic in life or work.

The expansion of this couples group idea so that twenty-five such groups were in existence by the end of a decade is not the whole of the story. The utilization of the small group as a caring fellowship even when gathered for teacher training, for adult study, for prayer, for boards and commissions, for training stewardship canvass workers and for working with young people, became typical in the life of this large congregation. In the course of a year over three hundred small groups, both transient and enduring, gathered for various purposes in the life of the church of 2200 members. In each of these the contribution of those who had learned what it means to care for others as persons was made. The leaven of Christian love was released through the whole of the body.

Intimacy, parents and purpose. The three crises of the contemporary marriage and family analyzed in Chapter One were spoken to directly by the Couples Christian Concern Groups. The gulf between husbands and wives was bridged by simply sitting them down in a circle with other husbands and wives and opening up for discussion the concerns which mattered to either. The group became an avenue through which husbands and wives could discover their partners as persons.

---

[6] Robert A. Edgar's account of this development is in the article, "The Listening Structured Group," in *Pastoral Psychology*, June, 1964.

John R. Fry attacks small groups in the church as being erotic societies which disrupt marriages. "Fetishlike openness and frankness provokes exactly the kind of spiritual undressing that cannot fail to have libidinous dimensions," he declares.[7] The fact of the matter is that the work of the couples groups actually decreases the problem of extramarital flight for sexual purposes. It does so by offering to those who have joined in marriage the opportunity of learning who it is one has so joined. It is a training in talking with one's partner about the real concerns of one's life rather than withholding these for various reasons of false chivalry. Any increase in the depth of intimacy between two persons already joined in sexual union strengthens that union by making it integrative of the whole of two persons. It is the marriage which has no growth in the intimate understanding and awareness of each other which stands precariously ready to topple into segmentalized sexual escapades. The paradoxical truth is that the direct assistance in the marital partners' understanding of each other as a person— training in intimacy even when conducted in a group setting— actually reduces the dangers of erotic cross-mating.

How is it that the group contributes to a marriage's growth in intimacy? It offers the forum of a group through which a partner may practice bringing up topics and issues which are of individual importance or which have been blocked in conflict when brought up between the partners alone.

Item: One husband who was working in a sales executive position glued to a desk wanted to discuss his dissatisfaction about it with his wife. Whenever he started to, the wife became deeply anxious over the prospect which a job-change would mean and would stop the discussion. She never knew therefore the depth of his unhappiness in not being in one of the regional sales positions until he used the group one evening to speak about this. The group was able to hear the wife in her anxieties and fears as well as the husband in his frustration. Through the willingness of the group members to hear out each of these two as persons, they made it possible for the couple to hear each other. The group served to open up communication and understanding between the marital couple which marriage counselors find they must do all the time. The group offered its *congregational care.* The couple ended this evening knowing of each other more fully than they ever had before. The next day the

---

[7] John R. Fry, *op. cit.,* p. 25.

husband did what he had wanted to do for years and had feared his wife would not understand. He confronted his boss with his desire to "step down" into a field sales position. He made it an ultimatum that either he would get the next such opening or he would look elsewhere. Within two months the opening came and this husband received it. The five years since making this change have brought the kind of happiness in his work which he had been denied for over five years previously because he never had really aired the issue with his wife.

Assembled statements from members of these concern groups corroborate their value for the marital relationship. One member testified, the group "helps my wife and I to talk about general problems and specific personal ones." Still another person found the group offered "new insight into one's mate's feelings." Another person jotted down this description of a group's meaning, "This is the only time my husband and I go out *together*." No doubt she was emphasizing the fact that numerous times when they go out they really are not together.

The second of the crises in the family, the crisis of parenthood, represents an anxious concern extending throughout the two decades of parenthood. The opportunity to raise with other parents the kinds of perplexities one confronts with one's own children is regularly utilized in these groups. When the group contains a mixture of parentage running from newly-weds to grandparents, wisdom is shared naturally. Grandparental wisdom coming from someone else is accepted in a way which the same kind of words from the grandparents of one's own children is not. The wisdom flows both ways. The new parent couple, a generation younger than the couple with the "empty nest," offer insight to grandparents regarding the mind and thought of their own children off in some other place. The hazards of joining different generations in a Christian Concern Group are not nearly so great as one might suppose from the perspective of the separation of generations which occurs within the family. Crossing family lines opens up communication which otherwise tends to be blocked.

The third of the family crises, the crisis of meaninglessness within contemporary man, is spoken to through the Couple Christian Concern Group by the way in which it opens couples to the pastoral care which the Gospel encountered in worship and study provides. The group working together catches a glimpse of the deeper search for meaning which Christians are entered upon. A statement from another participant puts the matter thus:

> The "thing" which impressed me most of all, and "helped" me most of all, was learning that others (most others) are just as perplexed, just as ignorant, just as confused, just as interested and just as searchingly interested in arriving at a "belief"—a real belief in God.

The group experience complements and commends the discipline of regular worship and study.

In the group, the "concerns" which husbands typically raise press the question of the meaning of the Gospel for issues and problems in the business world. The advertising executive questioning the ethical direction of practices in his own company asks for a rationale in the Gospel which extends to his plight. The discovery that the ambiguity of his existence, from which he is helpless to extricate himself, is that to which God's Word of forgiveness is addressed helps him in ways which surpass all personal helping.

The normative meaning of the Gospel for the life of each member is kept in tension with life issues as the group self-consciously asks "what does it mean to be 'Christian' in his circumstance?"

The new family. The small Christian fellowship becomes the new family in Christ. One of the continuing discoveries of participants in this kind of life together is that others who seem so strange and different share the same human predicaments. This is not immediately perceived. The first perceptions of members are filled with stereotyping of each other. Sometimes the categorizing is so strong that couples will think it impossible to return to a group because of a particular person encountered. At such a time the reminder is made that this group is not gathered just to enjoy one another. It is a gathering of persons who have their real unity not in their mutual acceptance but in Christ's acceptance of each. Through Christ what is unacceptable in another becomes acceptable. The task of the member becomes one of practicing this meaning of Christian love.

When the new family in Christ lives together for a while they discover that the other members of the group have become their new extended family. This is because bonds develop which go beyond common friendships. Such is the testimony of another long time participant in these groups:

The real value of the group is the personal concern we have for one another, a personal concern which goes beyond that of friendship and becomes almost familial. Thus a problem is treated with earnest, loving care, with consideration of the individual's own personality and the group aim is to help rather than to reform or inform.

Like a family, one enjoys a different kind of freedom to be oneself in this kind of group. Another person comments:

To me the Christian Concern Group is another 'family' where I can blow off steam and feel understood in the process.

In a society where the isolated conjugal family is the norm, the members of a small, caring fellowship discover the place of the extended family is taken by those to whom one is joined in the family of Christ.

Out of the sensitivities to others as persons worked toward in the Couples Concern Groups, there develops an awareness which feeds back into life relationships including those in one's own family. This is what happened for this person:

The most valuable personal value was my increased sensitivity to feelings, emotions, need to be understood, desire to be accepted, in other people—in the other groups with which I was connected. In some respects this presents a real problem. I was conscious of the bad group dynamics at every dinner table, at a family discussion, at an informal gab fest. I was often able to help—more often aware but out-numbered!

"Aware but out-numbered" and yet trying to do something about the other points of human encounter. A more human existence is seen as a challenge to the human gifts which have been given this person.

This sampling of statements gives some glimpse of the values which emerge in fostering the Couples Christian Concern Group. How does one set such groups in motion?

Pastoral Oversight

Initiating a group. The size of a group is happily kept at six couples. Sometimes a group of five couples or seven couples will be formed because there is just this number of couples available at a given moment. Twelve people represent a group which will have enough diversity of persons and still allow for each person to be a participating member in a "family" rather than simply one individual in a class.

A group is gathered by "pastoral hunch" and personal invitation. The pastor in his routine parish calling will find couples of seasoned maturity and couples of obvious immaturity. A group needs one of the former and the latter needs such a group. The pastor will find couples who are looking for a more serious religious obligation than worship on Sunday provides, yet hesitant and suspicious about the typical kinds of church organizational life. He will find couples new to the church and community who wish to "belong," couples who want "instant roots" to counteract their endless mobility. He will find couples of long years in the church who have come through some crisis to ask the more searching questions. He will find couples perplexed in their marriages and uncertain as parents, looking for help. He will find business people skeptical about the Christian enterprise, saying "show me" that Christianity is relevant.

The first meeting of the group in the parsonage living room or an informal room at the church offers the pastor the opportunity to be host and to demonstrate a new host's role relative to this kind of group. One of the mistakes of the usual host to a social group can be offset at the beginning. The purpose of this group is not to lead up to some refreshment display or competition. Coffee and simple cookies are served as soon as the group gathers. This avoids having the climactic event of the evening be the hostess' culinary preparations. Incidentally serving a light refreshment first permits the variations in time of arrival to be balanced out in an informal and "settling down" way. The "meeting" begins when all have arrived and have been introduced.

Then the first evening is given over to introductions in a fuller way. Each person is given five to ten minutes to describe the life pilgrimage which has been his or hers up to this point. This permits the one describing his own life situations to others to lift out what he considers the important circumstances of his life. One of the discoveries of this self-description is a new self-recognition. "Who am I?" and "What are my real goals?" tend to gain answers in this kind of brief autobiographical sketch. Those hearing this account begin to discover the person behind the appearance. But in a first time together, this is only a beginning.

Frequently when a group turns a year together they find it valuable to begin again. They return to an evening given over to brief autobiographies. This time the telling of the brief autobiography brings new facets of the person to each biographer and a new level of hearing is present in the group.

The experience as to frequency of group meeting is varied. We found that one meeting every other week was something couples could sustain on a long-term basis.

Setting a pattern for the group. New groups quickly develop the terms on which members will relate to one another. When one is dealing with a new group, new terms for group life can be introduced. If they are not introduced, then the group will utilize its prior experiences without reflection. The second evening is an important one. In a few brief remarks, the pastor can offer new terms on which this group will function. Here is a sample of what might be said:

"As a group for *couples,* we will consciously avoid the usual social segregation of conversation. We will speak about matters which may affect women or men more in any given time, but we will do so as people willing to bridge the chasm of the man's world and the woman's world.

"As *Christians* we seek the meaning of our Christian commitment in relationship to the issues under discussion. As *Christians* we also will practice Christian love for the neighbor in this very group. This requires new skill in listening to others and in seeking to enter the world of someone different from ourselves. As *Christians* we shall expect to remain sinners, preferring our own view of things, rejecting the communication and the person of others, and being insensitive. Thus to be *Christian* involves struggle which will take place in the very exchanges within this group. It is the struggle of the 'good that I would do, I do not' and 'that which I would not, I do.' This group provides a laboratory for the experimentation with new ways to cope with the sin of self, new ways to test 'a more excellent way.' As *Christians* we can take up the work of 'bearing one another's burdens.' As *Christians* we shall learn our ministry of pastoral care in this group.

"As *concerned* Christians we will explore the peculiar point in our own existence where we find the greatest difficulty in being a

Christian man or a Christian woman. We speak of *concerns* in order to avoid giving the impression that we will be talking only about personal problems. We are not gathered to be a therapy group for disturbed individuals. Yet we will be helpful to persons without trying to be analysts. *Concerns* is a word which also suggests the broadest possible issues of the Christian faith in relation to the world may appropriately fix our attention.

"To gather concerns I am passing out a blank 3 by 5 card for you to use individually to write down a sample 'concern' of yours. After we have taken a few minutes to reflect, these will be gathered and I will go over whatever is written down as a spokesman for the group. We shall choose among these concerns the one or two which speak most directly to all of us or which issue with the most urgent ring. As we develop we shall grow in our ability to sense the focal concerns for an evening."

It is sometimes possible to have a group offer their concerns verbally going around the circle in turn. Those wishing to do so, will pass. But this verbal form of beginning to gather the concerns for a given evening is usually better used later in a group's life than earlier.

Here is a sample of what actually appeared the first time such an opportunity was extended to a group of laymen to write down their concerns within the context just described:

You hear a great deal about "where are we going?" This is a very individualized answer but isn't it something that should be considered. What would you like to see accomplished for yourself in five or ten years?

How to reconcile the "Christian way of life" with competitive demands of business.

How does one go about changing a Sunday School curriculum without making those in present supervision think that the desire is purely critical.

Alcoholism—cause or effect.

How can we each develop a closer personal relationship with God and really feel and use the power available to us?

What do you do with yourself when you're under "pressure?"

Is Church membership a "must" for Christianity?

To what extent should the family supplement in the home the church's teachings.

How do we really feel about minority groups and our so-called "restricted village"? Are we ready to practice inter-mingling?

Nine out of twelve cards were written on. This is a typical percentage. The pastor then read this list over slowly to the group twice. The group chose the second one to talk about first, bowing to the voice of several men which chorused in on the conflict between Christianity and the aggressive competitiveness of their business life. The last suggested topic was probably too hot to handle on a first round (this being only the second evening), but it can safely be assumed to be a near priority issue. It is one which the group will get to simply because of the urgency of issues of northern segregation for a suburban community. The discussion on the chosen concern is opened up by the one who wrote the concern. The response of others may elaborate, explore, question, clarify, match the situation described, etc.

The pastor is but one member of the group when the discussion gets underway. He is, hopefully, more sensitive to the quality of the communication which is taking place. He is not there to dominate or to see that the "right" solution emerges. When there is a question which his theological perspective and training can clarify, he will offer his understanding. But it is important for him to avoid *ex cathedra* pronouncements. His is an opportunity to add the thinking of one Christian to the issues as they emerge; when he does this he helps the group sense the meaning of the Christian norm which they may bring to bear at any future point in their life together.

Ways of self-observation. The third contribution of the pastor to the formation of groups for congregational care is a variety of means by which the group can become sensitive to its working as a group.

The simplest means of all is *reserving the last five minutes* of the evening for the group to look back at its group behavior during the evening. Asking for members to volunteer their unskilled observations usually yields several which give the group some sense of where they have been and how they have measured up to their Christian task. If they have not practiced trying to understand the person who presents a concern, the one person who will make this perfectly clear is the holder of the concern. If no one has brought the question under the perspective of a Christian faith, noting this is important.

Another way to assist the group to be aware of its life as a group is to utilize a *companion observer* for an evening. The observer comes not as an intruder but as a companion in this venture in congregational care whose home base is a similar group.

One avenue of helping the group to be an observer of itself is for the *pastor to return* to the group after it has been underway for three or four months without his presence. At such a time he slips into the group as an interested observer and can help by offering his observations toward the end of the evening of how the group is functioning. There is no way to avoid the fact that the use of a companion group observer or of the pastor as a returnee to the group he was with at the start introduces the possibility that the group will be conscious of itself being observed. The check upon this is the fact that the participants in the group are observers also. The use of an outsider will help evoke the participants' observations and these can be given the greater weight.

When a number of groups are functioning simultaneously, pastoral oversight in helping the groups can come through a *resource meeting*. During one year we held resource meetings every other month and had a different couple from each group at each meeting. In a twelve-month period nearly every couple in twenty-five groups had attended one of these training evenings. In the meeting there was exchange of information about the different groups and training in the process of listening. This was a time to look at process without distracting the normal group's primary focus upon Christian concerns. In this special meeting we took a look at process separate from the group meetings themselves.

Still another resource is the *parish life conference*. This is a weekend retreat-conference used for the purpose of helping church school teachers become sensitive to the phenomena of group behavior. For Concern Group Members it has the same values.

Care in the Laymen's Hands

Shared leadership. The role of host which rotates from house to house provides a natural basis for shifting the responsibility of chairing the meeting from the pastor's shoulders after the first two sessions to the host of the evening. He can convene the meeting, circulate blank cards on which to place concerns, assist the group in making a choice of one or two concerns for use in a given evening, help the group to shift to the next concern when a natural break comes and provide some review of the group's way of working in the last five minutes of the evening.

Apart from these convening and chairing functions which will rotate easily, the leadership functions provided when individuals in the group are listened to, supported and understood, when the group's task is focused and contributed to, and when the group's working relations are facilitated, will emerge from the members of the group itself.

The real significance of the shared leadership which this kind of caring fellowship provides is the way in which pastoral care in the form of real help to persons as persons is provided. When the person is treated with desire to "help rather than to reform or to inform," the potentials of care in the hands of the congregation are quickly realized.

Examples of congregational care. Practically every group in time comes to be a source of excellent pastoral care for each of the members of the group. In some circumstances of special need, groups have functioned with a ministry of pastoral care which is equal, if not superior, to that available from a specialized ministry of pastoral counseling.

Item. One group which had been working together as a Concern Group for over four years provided to one couple in particular a continuing resource for a marriage which was repeatedly threatened. The warfare and fighting which existed between the husband and wife was brought into the open within the group time and time again. The other members of the group felt the seriousness of the quarreling and responded with their care to both of the partners as persons. Fortunately one couple in the group was a full generation older and served with natural therapeutic skills as permissive, helping parents. Other couples more nearly represented siblings who were ready to help but were not about to live another's life for either one. The existence of a couple in strife within any typical social group usually disrupts such a group. This couple clearly placed a strain upon the Concern Group at times. But the group maintained its strengthening and supportive life for this couple for well over four years in my personal knowledge. They knew they were gathered to show forth the light of Christ and not just to run when the darkness deepened.

It might be argued that the troubled couple would have been better helped to go to a specialist and not take so much time of so many. Yet, they were not the exclusive preoccupation of this group's time. The group was the arena to which their frequent marital crises were brought when they occurred. At other times this couple was a part of the pastoral care extended to others in the group.

Lest it be thought that this was a group which exacted all the energies of five couples to support through pastoral care the one couple, let me indicate that every person in the group carried some work or office in the church. Several were leaders of community service activities including the husband of the troubled couple. One other wife was in a post-hospital phase of adjustment from a serious mental illness. To her the group was serving as a place of return to the community in the finest way possible—almost incidentally in relation to the struggles of the marital discord couple.

Item. Another group found that it was the family and the pastor to one of its members when a tragic automobile accident killed outright the wife and mother of three who had been in their group for four years. During the hospital period and long convalescence which the husband went through following the accident which killed his wife, the Concern Group responded directly and naturally as a burden-bearing body, sustaining this husband in his loss and in his slow recovery. The years of the group's life together prior to the accident built the kind of bonds which enabled ten other people to be concerned Christians in the midst of one of their number's grief and recovery from fractures. The group was the pastoral reality to this man more than the pastor could be.

Item. In the suburban community we found another form of need existing which the couple structure of our concern groups tended to overlook for a time. This is the problem of the widow who remains in the community after the premature death of her husband. The burden of the whole of parenthood is thrust upon her. The opportunity to talk things over with an adult companion is severely restricted. We found that it was possible to include a widow within the membership of a number of groups. This was far superior to making widows a special case and forming a group for them alone. The couples group in accepting the widow into their midst did so with compassion but not condescension. They truly exercised the charity which may be expected of a Christian and proved another way in which the care of the congregation extends itself naturally once channels of such care are opened.

Item. There are many persons who come to seek help from a pastor at times of distress in their lives. They do not become extended interview cases chiefly because the problem is acute and transitory. One conversation usually affords the perspective and relief which is needed. In the ten years of my knowledge of the working of the Couples Christian Concern Groups I can testify to the reality of the pastoral care embedded within the congregation by these groups by the fact that no appeals for acute, momentary help came from members of these groups! The groups themselves were the resource of this kind of pastoral care. Frequently more chronic problems would be opened to light sufficiently so that an individual would seek additional specialized pastoral counseling. But the temporary crises were met and helped through the care offered by the groups themselves.

The Lay Apostolate

One of the great chasms which confronts church life in our times is the way in which the Christian faith has become something apart from life. How to move the Gospel beyond the church walls and into the world is a critical matter. If there will be any heralds of the gospel beyond church building walls, they will be laymen. But typically something more is needed beyond church membership and church attendance before the layman comes to see his life in the world as mission on behalf of Christ. The forming of Couples Christian Concern Groups makes five important contributions to this end. (1) It forms the church in the house and so breaks open a new image of the church beyond the building. (2) It cultivates the conversation of Christians and prepares them for conversation with the world. (3) It provides times of discernment and reflection on what God requires of us now. (4) It rehearses the reconciling work of the Christian which is to be his ministry in the world. (5) And it provides a natural group for adult study.

The house church. The use of the living room of church families for the sake of being the church gathered tells the members something about the scattered thrust of the church. The Gospel is to go to our homes, families and daily vocations. When it does the church is alive through its members to being the church in the world. The concern groups make the church a new reality for their members in the gathering of Christians for thought and reflection as Christians in household settings. A part of the chasm between the church and world is bridged. Even when the most convenient and appropriate place for the group to meet is in a room at the church the nature of the conversation symbolizes movement of the mutual ministry from the churchly to the worldly sphere.

Christian conversation. Some of the appeals for change in the introversive character of the church tend to suppose that exhortation alone will effect the change. The great gulf between the Christain style of life and the ways of the world is not so easily transcended. Ordinary Christians need an awful lot of talking with each other as Christians if they are to put on "the mind of Christ." D. T. Niles has suggested that the Gospel needs to be so commonplace that people would "gossip" it around. In the small couples groups we have been describing, a good deal of what is taking place is just this commonplace "gossiping of the Gospel." Many scholars react with fright to groups which are not structured to provide hard lessons in Biblical subjects. They view them as "the pooling of ignorance." Our response to this is twofold. At the level of knowing the imperative of the Gospel, the ordinary gathering of Christians is not so ignorant! At the level of increasing their Biblical understanding they need motivation to study more than anything else. Conversation among Christians with respect to their concerns as Christians in the world helps both to initiate a new style of Christian life and to open up the desire and hunger for Biblical understanding of this life style.

That the conversation moves beyond the personal is testified to by the following statement from a group member:

Talking about problems of the persons involved is important but these are evaluated against "What a Christian should do."

It is this conversation about being a Christian which is needed to form a new mind-set for the Christian community with which it may withstand the erosions of Christian belief in contemporary culture.

Theological reflection and discernment. The reliance upon the sermon to lift up the Word of God in relation to the issues of our common life can only go so far in an increasingly specialized technological world. The conversation of the layman about the meaning of the gospel for his life requires new ways for laymen to speak to each other in the light of the Word. Not all the discerning of the meaning of God's Word and not all the reflection upon God's relation to the particular man which we desire as pastors will come from what transpires in the pew on Sunday. One of the great values of the Christian Concern Group in the parish is that it becomes a place where the Word of God pointed to in the sermon is explored afresh. Some of the meat of a good sermon is served to the conversation of these groups of Christians gathering on alternate weeks.

Thus the concerns of the Christian in these groups arise from two different directions: from the thrust of preaching in the church and from the issues of life and vocation. The group discussion more often than not is the place where a theological glimpse of an existential situation is gained. The layman learns to discern through reflection which is generated by the theological insights of a sermon what it is that God may require of him now.

Item. The advertising agency owner who brought his concern about the terms of competition with one particular competitor confronted the prospect of providing call girls as well as hotel accommodations for his clients or risk the loss of clients to a competitor who was doing this. The imperative of the Gospel in his partcular circumstance seemed a costly one. But as he reflected upon what business he would really be engaged in if he decided to match his competition, a revulsion welled within himself far more commanding than a preached admonition would have been at that particular moment. The cost of business lost on such terms he was ready to reckon a small one. The group provided the occasion for reflection upon and discernment of what was requred of him in his ministry in the world.

Rehearsal for reconciliation. A constant tension in a concern group exists between the acceptance of others as persons and all the myriad forms of alienation which infect the human mind and heart. It takes practice to learn to accept a neighbor, much less care about him. The closed fellowship of a small group offers a place to practice acceptance, to experience it from others, and to offer it to the one whom you would be tempted to withhold it from. This becomes a work of learning which gains its greatest lessons in confronting the divisions and alienations of class and race. It is to these divisions of the world that the Christian is sent forth to exercise his reconciling agency.

The rhythm of adult study. The kind of group we have been speaking about is a continuing group set up as one of the disciplines of church membership. Adult study is forwarded in time-limited periods and for this reason programs in the fall and spring running for five to eight weeks are a frequent part of church life today. We found that the offering of significant Biblical study and study of important social issues were properly placed in these Fall and Lenten schools. The concern groups were encouraged and tended to register for courses as a group. Then they would hold a discussion each night following the course among themselves as a ready-made discussion group. After the fall or Lenten period of weekly study was concluded they would resume their schedule of meeting every other week. The limited periods of study in the fall and spring supplemented the lack of reliance upon "resource material" within the normal life of the group. There was a helpful alternation between intensive study in the fall and in the spring and the ongoing existence of the group as a concern group.

The net effect of the kind of nurture and congregational care which we have pointed to is that it was equipping the Christian man or woman to be a Christian in his place of work and witness in the world. Not nurture instead of mission, but nurture so that mission will truly occur.

Problems and Cautions

Many pastors having heard about the boons which small group life will bring for the renewal of church life, have tried to use this idea—at least their understanding of this idea. The encounter with problems arising with these new forms has burnt the fingers of many. They back away pronouncing anathema upon them and saying they have given small groups a try. Some alerting of the reader to the problems in small group life is needed in order to prevent hasty advocacy by anyone of what we are suggesting.

Slow development not crash programs. One denomination has recently decreed that every congregation should reorder itself into small group patterns. This is surely the route to disaster. Unless pastors themselves grow in an understanding and sensitivity to the problems and potentials of the small *koinonia* group through experience in one they will not attend to the problems of oversight which we have enumerated as the pastor's continuing responsibility. The discovery of the pastor's contribution to the success of a true *koinonia* group is the discovery of a different role than just organizing an officer led, age-sex social gathering under church auspices.

The testimony of every current report including this one on the discovery of the meaning of the small group for the renewal of the congregation is one of simple beginnings. It is better to organize a single group for a year and let it succeed in the kinds of purposes we have been outlining than to spread one's efforts thin in order to quickly seize the kingdom. A mustard-seed approach is in order.

One of the reasons for a humble beginning is the retraining of the pastor in his role as an auxiliary to the ministry of the laity. Another reason is that claims for the values of such a group are effectively made by those who have come to realize these values, not by exhortation. It is right that a successful experience in Christian caring should become "good news" which others are eager to hear and desirous of sharing themselves.

Seeding rather than fission. The launching of a second group poses the problem of whether to divide those who have come to share the values of this life together as Christians in order to have a second group, or to leave it intact. Leaving it intact will be necessary if a truly significant life of mutual ministry has been established. The avenue of approach to a second group which we used successfully was to ask a spiritually mature couple from the original group to undertake a six-month "mission" assignment as the resource couple for another group. Their continued participation in their own group is not disrupted. The new group knows that this couple with experience is "on loan" for a beginning period only. The new group is seeded with the best of experience and insight into the values, functions and purposes of this Christian life together.

A style of life not a short course. The kind of congregational care we are proposing is mistaken if it is seen as a short-course idea of fixed duration. The time-limited group operates under hazards which will prevent its discovery of the sustaining effect of Christian upon Christian which comes in the long-term commitment to a group. It is preferable to see what we are proposing as one of the disciplines of church life for the modern church rather than as one of the study programs of the church school. It requires a commitment of membership beyond church attendance, giving, service in the church and service in the community. It is a commitment in mutual care which undergirds the entire life of the body both to strengthen its church-directed ministeries and its world-directed ministries. Seen in this light it becomes a part of the Christian style of life. Without mutual care, the Christian life is lopsided.

Searching for Christian witness not psychic séances. Some of the fears which are dredged up whenever one speaks of small groups is that these will become places of "spiritual undressing" and psychic disrobing. Unfortunately there have been cell group ideas in the past which have placed a premium upon moral and spiritual excellence as though it were about to be achieved in the small group—confessional style. The task of the group is not simply the nursing of psychic sensitivity. There is nurture; there is caring; and there is growth in sensitivity to the person behind the *persona*. But these are functions of the group as a group learning to show mutual care. The task of the group is a different matter. "What does it mean to be a Christian in this or that problem or issue?" This is the question which defines the task of the group. It is a group searching for the meaning of the Christian Gospel in the vortex of life pressures. The task of the group is thus objective to the group life itself; objective both in the sense that the Gospel stands over against each individual Christian and in the sense that the life vocations of the members stand external to the group.

It will be obvious that even when one is successful in establishing the Christian Concern Group as a form of congregational care and as a place of searching for the Christian witness to the world, there will be many members of a typical church who will not have the least interest in this form of the Christian life. At this point one can only stress the great amount of work to be done for and with those who are ready to take their discipleship more seriously in this way. This is enough to occupy several pastors in most congregations.

A group for mutual growth not a psychiatric catch-all. In speaking about this form of congregational care in a volume in a pastoral counseling series, we should caution against any one's supposing that these groups of ordinary church members can be set up as therapy groups for the seriously disturbed. The problems of group therapy are such as to require a good therapist. We are not arguing for that kind of care which requires the permanent presence even of the pastor. Rather we assume the pastor may remove himself from a group after it has established itself. In initiating a group the pastor should avoid putting more than one seriously disturbed couple in any given group. The clustering of all the "problem people" of a parish in one group will defeat the purpose of creating a form of mutual care in which the average person needs help. One formula which we found helpful was that of being sure that a "natural" therapeutic person or couple were added to each group in which a seriously disturbed person was placed. Extra strength in maturity of one counter-balanced the added immaturity of the other.

Replacements, termination and regrouping. The high mobility of our society militates against the long-term group anywhere. In the forming of one group we had the experience of losing three couples through transfers between the first and second meeting of the group. Obviously, it was necessary to start all over again with the remaining three couples. Usually losses to a group occur one couple at a time.

The initial loss to a group may come when the group has met for three times. The initial commitment asked of each couple joining a group is that they decide whether to stay in a group after meeting three times with the group rather than after the first night. This reduces the loss through aversions to stereotypes of strangers.

It permits the person to see some of the constructive use of such a group experience. Occasionally a couple will choose not to continue in the group on the basis of this three-time trial. When this happens the adding of a replacement couple to bring the group to six couples can be done. Sometimes the initial trial group will include seven couples just to allow for the possibility of one couple's withdrawal on a graceful basis.

When a new couple is added to an existing group, the only caution to express is that of helping them start on a similar footing. This is done by having the group meet again in the parsonage living room or the church and using the brief autobiographies as the format of the evening again. This tells the new couple that all are meeting each other for the first time—for the first time with that couple.

Occasionally a group may need to schedule a termination date as the means of breaking with a pattern which has proved obstructive to the mission and purpose of these groups. The use of the end of the year before summer vacations is a convenient and natural stopping point. However it is necessary for the group itself to see that its way of functioning is a faulty one. One way in which this can be accomplished is through the group *resource meeting*, mentioned earlier. The exercise of pastoral oversight means that there are times when the pastor needs to risk offending by urging a group to disband. The actual dynamic in the group is that a pattern of operation other than the one which will be fruitful has come into play. Let me suggest two such patterns.

Item. One group had admitted a couple who were not church members as a kind of missionary venture. The couple turned out to hold deep and persistent antagonisms to any form of explicit Christian faith as well as to all organized expressions of the church. They did not see this group as a form of the life of the church. The members of the group attempted to exercise their reconciling work by studiously avoiding "Christian" issues. This was failing. Setting a terminal date beyond which only those who wanted to join in different groups would go was decided upon. The outside couple did not want to go on to life within the congregation as a part of Christian commitment. Their loyalty, it turned out, was to a particular couple in the group who had invited them in the first place. This regrouping of the whole by termination of the old group permitted this pattern of "least common faith" to be broken.

Item. Another group was functioning as an expression of the religious interests of only one of its members. This member was a woman of truly remarkable, charismatic gifts. To all intents and purposes it seemed that each meeting of this group was an unusual time of Christian searching and testimony. As a matter of fact it was far too spiritually pure for the misgivings, doubts and problems of the members of the group to appear. Yet the group did not dissolve because the real charisma of its central member gave some sustenance to each member. What the other members were not gaining was growth in the exercise of their own Christian response and sense of responsibility. The transfer of this dominant couple out of town provided a question of either terminating the group or adding in a new member couple. In choosing the former alternative we believed that the pattern of the old group had been set so much in terms of the gifted woman who had dominated it that more was to be gained by dividing the group and sending its remnant members as replacements to other groups lacking one couple. These transferred members quickly discovered a strangely different potential of the group than they had known.

The pastor's own family. We have suggested two different things as we have described the pastor's relationship to the group. Now we shall add a third. On the one hand we have suggested that the pastor need only stay with a group until it is established in the pattern indicated. This is usually a period of four to six sessions. On the other hand we have suggested that the beginning of this form of congregational care ought to be slow and that the pastor himself needs to learn how to step aside and become a member of a group. The third thing we have to say is that the pastor and his wife ought to belong to one group as an ordinary member for the sake of their own family, marriage and personal need. Obviously each of these suggestions would be hard to effect with one and the same group.

A long-term relationship with one group in which the pastor and his wife are members on a common footing with other members may be achieved in relation to the first group formed whose slow and successful development he can carefully follow out of the non-ordinary member corner of his eye. In the forming of additional groups his role is limited to those functions belonging to pastoral oversight.

The need of the pastor for some place where he and his wife meet other Christians as struggling believers in the midst of a company of such is very great. The loneliness of the ministry is haunting and overwhelming when the relationship with other Christians is always that of pastor to people. The ministry of the laity in pastoral care can include ministry to a pastor through the group pattern we have been advocating. The need of his wife for this kind of sustaining fellowship equals her husband's need.

There will be those who believe it is not possible for the pastor to be one member of his congregation even in a Couples Christian Concern Group. To be sure there are aspects of his role as leader of the whole congregation which inevitably adhere, but the belief in the fundamentally equal footing of every Christian as a sinner in need of God's grace indicates an equality which his pastoral role never obliterates. In the light of this equality of all sinners before God and the priesthood of all believers through the one great priestly work of Christ, the ministry of pastoral care in the congregational group can be mutual even when the pastor is one member of such a group.

We have described a form of pastoral care belonging to the members of the congregation which meets a variety of needs. The needs of marriage and the family in our time are met in part by this congregational care. The need to activate in new forms the life of Christian work and witness is met also. Within this general matrix of a ministering congregation, the pastor's extraordinary care to individuals may be forwarded without ostrichlike oblivion to the needs of many. But even individual pastoral care may be in need of some review and reappraisal. The balance of our attention in his volume is turned to one such area of reappraisal—work with family problems.

Part II

FAMILY COUNSELING

CHAPTER THREE

PERSONS In FAMILIES

Perspectives on Personality

The relation of personality theory and helping procedures.
The way in which help is offered to a person is a function of one's
understanding of personality. In broadest terms the understanding
of what man is has a controlling effect upon all healing work. This
relationship is readily seen in ages other than our own.

Pre-scientific theory of personality in the West (and in most folk
cultures) accounted for behavior deviation by positing demonic
spirits which took possession of the deviate person. On this basis,
the treatment of the trouble was either by removing the demon-
filled person from human contact so that contamination of others
was avoided or by exorcising the demons. These two treatments are
contrasted in the gospel account of Jesus' encounter with the
Gerasene demoniac (Luke 8:26–40).

In the age of rationalism, the person was understood in terms of
the dominance of the mind within the organism. Even so, loss of
mindedness was accounted for by alien spirit possession, hence the
asylums for the mentally deranged in the 19th century were built
as medieval fortresses in remote places locking the spirit possessed
away from the world. However, reliance upon rational forms of
treatment—advice, admonition, persuasion, exhortation—occurred
wherever reason remained. Mild behavior deviations met rational
correctives. Reason was presumed to reign supreme among a cluster
of faculties in man. To be in possession of one's faculties was to
be under the control of reason.

Whatever the theory of the person, it is important. From it flows
the way a society will deal with disturbances in human behavior.
An incredible thrust of the genius of Sigmund Freud gave modern

man both a new glimpse of what it means to be a human personality and a new approach to helping people. (43) In the wake of the Freudian revolution other theories of human nature have modified and even competed with Freud's. The most significant modification to Freud's theory of personality offered by both psychoanalytic deviationists and other psychologists is a new awareness of the social dimension in personality.

The fresh appreciation of the social dimension in personality in turn has begun to effect radical changes in procedures of psychotherapists. When the social context of personality is taken with high seriousness in personality theorizing it leads to a changed appreciation of social reality in psychotherapeutic work. From countless quarters these changes in treatment work are including the *family* in the psychotherapeutic process.

Building on the ground swell of these new advocates of psychotherapy with the family, we shall outline an adaptation applicable to pastoral work with families.

The Freudian perspective on personality. The longtime inability of modern psychotherapists to work in any way other than with the single individual in isolation or with a group of individuals only when each is isolated from his normal social reality now seems strange. But the model of clinical isolation of the individual for psychotherapeutic work has prevailed as a direct consequence of the half-century of dominance of Freudian personality theory. Within this theory, the root explanatory constructs were individualized forces. The corresponding approach to treatment was accordingly individualized.

In expanding the self-awareness of man from the rational-observable to include the irrational-hidden, Freud posited a biological force as the basic entity in man's psychic life. He called this force the libido. By this term Freud gave to instinct-theory a new breadth and scope of interpretative value for human self-understanding. But at the same time he sided with the biologically given within the spectrum of biological and social realities comprising individual existence. The bias in favor of the biological within Freudian theory is disclosed in Freud's location of instinct in bodily excitation.

An instinct may be described as having a source, an object and an aim. The source is a state of excitation within the body, and its aim is to remove that excitation; in the course of its path from its source to the attainment of its aim the instinct becomes operative mentally.[1]

The physiological residence of instinct conditions the attention given in psychoanalysis and subsequent psychotherapeutic work to the isolated individual.

It might be argued that Freud took adequate cognizance of the social forces shaping personality because his theory of libidinal development really traces the relation of the infant to the mother in the nursing period, in the phase of toilet training, in the early attachments of childhood, etc. However, the dominant reality in Freud's theory was not what was taking place in the social transactions, but rather what was unfolding in the instinctual-biological sphere. Thus each of the major Freudian stages of personality development has a bodily, organismic name not an interpersonal one; oral, anal and phallic stages not nursing, training and adult social participation periods.

Still another way of gauging the bias toward the biological and hence the discrete individual organism in Freud's personality theory is seen in his choice of language for describing the organized functioning of the individual. The ego and the super-ego (two borrowers of energy from the id) together with the instinctual id, define the various mental manifestations of the primal psychic energy. The fact that Freud never uses the term "self" to describe the organized functioning of personality indicates the low significance which transactions of the individual with other individuals had for his theory of personality. Freud restricts his view of personality to the biologically grounded id-ego-super-ego.

Interpersonal theory of personality. By the time Percival Symonds wrote his essay on *The Ego and the Self* (44), dividing Freud from the neo-Freudians, almost fifteen years of writing from psychoanalytic deviationists such as Karen Horney, Erich Fromm, and Harry Stack Sullivan had accumulated. Each of these authors,

---

[1] Sigmund Freud, *A New Series of Introductory Lectures to Psychoanalysis* (New York: W. W. Norton & Company, Inc., 1933), pp. 132–133.

and even Alfred Adler with his earlier concept of the "life style" of the individual, sought a larger recognition in personality theory for the place of the social experiences of the individual. Each of them found the confines of the concept of the ego too restrictive. They opted for speaking of personality in terms of the "self." By this choice they assert that the response of the infant organism to its human environment was every bit as significant for human personality as whatever biological drives it may have.

Sullivan's understanding of anxiety puts the case clearly. Sullivan posits two different tension systems in the equipment of the human organism. One of these systems he describes as tensions of need. Various physiological requirements and safety requirements of existence comprise the tensions of need. When these needs are met the organismic deficiencies are satisfied. The second of the tension systems is spoken of as tensions of anxiety. The arousal of these tensions and their reduction occurs only in relation to the interpersonal environment. Other human beings excite or allay the tensions of anxiety. To enhance the organism's survival in the human environment the individual develops a "self-dynamism" which functions to keep anxiety to a minimum. The self-dynamism, powered by the tensions of anxiety, is an interpersonal phenomenon, not a biological endowment. Through memory and foresight it seeks out the feelings of security which come when the tensions of anxiety are allayed or reduced. In severe and traumatic circumstances of extreme anxiety, the self-dynamism rescues the organism from intolerable tensions through outright blocking of attention to the trauma-producing circumstance.

The self-dynamism, according to Sullivan, is a secondary motivational system which comes into existence in relation to the organism's encounter with other human beings. This dimension of humanity is not just an increment along some evolutionary scale, but it is a significant qualitative difference in human experiencing over and beyond the existence of our animal nature. By his one genus postulate, "everyone is much more simply human than otherwise,"[2] Sullivan emphasizes the distinctive qualitative change which participation in the human environment means for every

---

[2] Harry Stack Sullivan, *The Interpersonal Theory of Psychiatry* (New York: W. W. Norton & Company, Inc., 1953), p. 52.

human being, even for those with the least in native intellectual powers.

Mead and the self. Contemporaneously with Sullivan, but from the discipline of philosophy and social psychology rather than psychoanalytic psychiatry another seminal mind, George Herbert Mead, traced the meaning of selfhood within human existence. His views are so crucial for the "self-psychology" now flourishing and for the significance attaching to social experience in the organization of personality, we must note them as another force contributing to the break beyond Freud in the understanding of human personality.

Mead's preoccupation with the nature of the distinctively human led him to see a common phenomenon at work in the mindedness of man, the selfhood of man and the social existence of man. This phenomenon is the process of objectification requiring the ability to simultaneously stand and to transcend the immediate stance. This transcending or abstractive capacity is at the root of mind, self and society. Relative to the self which he defined as the individual's capacity to be an object to itself,[3] the transcending quality or capacity in man gives to man an objectification of his own behavior in the process of living with other human beings.

The gift of selfhood is not in the capacity for transcendence or objectification as a biological given, but in the exercise of that biological capacity through interaction with other persons. The milieu of such social interaction for the infant he located primarily in vocal gestures issuing in language or significant symbolic processes of exchange. The process of hearing one's own utterances and seeing another's behavior with respect to these is a primitive infant reflexive grasp of its own behavior. It is a beginning of the exercise of the capacity to be an object to oneself which is selfhood. Language interaction issuing into role patterns exercised in the seemingly innocent play of a child is a prototypical sample of self-behavior in later organized social roles.

Mead's attempt to identify the self as a participating product of the social process issued from a radical social behaviorism. At a time when Freud had revived instinct theory, Mead was working

---

[3] George Herbert Mead, *Mind, Self and Society* (Chicago: University of Chicago Press, 1934), p. 136.

out a conception of personality without any residual element of instinct. The biological component which he allowed and relied upon was quite the opposite of blind instinct, namely the capacity for self-transcendence inherent in objectification as a human social process. Mead elevated the social experience of the human to a position of importance with the same singlemindedness which Freud had shown in glorifying the explanatory power of instinct within the human. Though a contemporary of Freud's, the influence of Mead has been subsequent to Freud's primarily because of Mead's limited publication during his lifetime. All but one of his books are posthumous editings of class lectures by his former students. The influence of self-theory for personality thinking has been worked out only in the past three decades.

More important for our purposes is the fact that only in the past ten years have we begun to see influences of this socially enlarged understanding of personality to which the interpersonal theorists in psychiatry and Mead in social psychology contributed appearing in new forms of psychotherapeutic work. The appearance of these new ideas is one of the more exciting ferments in the present world of psychotherapy.

The Family as the Matrix of Persons

Marriage as an interpersonal contract. In the light of social theory of the self we find that the boundaries of personhood are difficult to establish wherever lives interact continually. When a new family is initiated at the time of marriage a new matrix for the existence of the person comes into being. The coming of children within a marriage creates a family system of interpersonal relationships. Thereafter it is difficult to see the person without seeing the family as a constellation in which each star is set.

One of the steps toward seeing the balance between persons existing in the family has been the discovery of the way in which marriage itself is a balancing of two complementary personalities. Several authors have recently suggested that marriage involves the choice of a mate whose neurotic tendencies complement one's own neurotic ways. (53) An ironic illustration of this is the genuine grief and loss felt by a wife over the death of a husband with whom she quarreled every day of her marriage. The importance of attack and counterattack for her own well-being was concealed even from herself by the smokescreen of the daily warfare. Apart from the stormy marriage, one finds various kinds of tranquility in marriage are frequently purchased by the pairing of opposite emotional patterns. Tendencies of one mate to dominate match well with needs of the other to be passive and submissive. But at subtler levels the interweaving of two self-systems bent upon reducing and avoiding anxiety means that many an accommodation of one person to another comes at the incipience of threatening gestures. The mutual accommodation goes on without surface evidence of anything happening.

The fact that some balance is struck between two persons in a marriage has led to new approaches in marital counseling which depart from strictly individualized approaches. There was a time not too distant when recommendations for marriage counseling stressed the necessity of the counselor seeing each partner separately (and preferably by separate counselors). Much of this is changing now under the impact of ideas about the dynamic balancing of security operations which takes place in mate selection and within the marriage. Increasingly we find that counseling with both the husband and wife together as a unit is being utilized for marital problems. The sharp reversal of a prior trend leads one therapist to assert, "In our clinic Staff presentations of new cases we almost feel a need to show cause why a patient should be treated individually, when he or she is married."[4] If marriage is a dynamic interpersonal reality for its partners, the same truth holds for the family and its members, particularly its younger members.

The family as an interpersonal balance.   There is a growing literature which describes the dynamic functioning of the family as a unity. Early psychoanalytic attention to this matter was offered by Alfred Adler. He first suggested that birth order was a significant factor in the developing life-style of each individual. A latter day Adlerian has recently spelled out an elaborate theory of birth order significance for personality extending to the ordinal position and

---

[4] John Warkentein, "President's Letter," *Newsletter of the American Academy of Psychotherapists,* Vol. 5, No. 1 (June 1960, p. 2).

sex of parental and grandparental generations.[5] Implicit in this theorizing is the idea that fairly stable role expectations adhere to various positions of a child within a family group and that these patterns persist into the parents' life with each other and with their own children.

A study by Hess and Handel describes five different patterns of family life which illustrate that "all families develop unique interactional patterns.[6] These unique interactional patterns are family themes or central concerns of a family with regard to its own existence as a family. Each member holds an image of himself, others and the family itself which revolves around its special theme. As a descriptive study assessing typical families functioning without disturbance to the communities in which they live, Hess and Handel are convinced that there is a unique interpersonal *system* in each family.

Other studies have sought to establish the concept of the pathognomic family. Erika Chance reported a research effort directed toward this end, based upon psychotherapeutic treatment given to mother and father as well as the "problem" child in a Philadelphia clinic. While not able to establish the concept of the pathognomic family, she did find "that the mother's concerns acted as a 'regulator' for the father and the child in specific areas."[7] Certain kinds of passively hostile mothers brought on similar characteristics in the fathers. Mothers preoccupied with the need for love, affection, and advice tended to restrict the child's ability to express such needs. While this study did not establish constellations of family illness, it did reveal two instances in which the mothers emotional functioning was shaping the emotional life of fathers or children.

At a theoretical level, Walter Garre (47), has made an arresting case for the family as the developer of its mentally ill member. Family members protect themselves against the "basic anxiety" evoked through any nuance of hostility by requiring one of their number to

---

[5] See Walter Toman, *Family Constellations*. (49)

[6] Robert D. Hess, and Gerald Handel, *Family Worlds, A Psychosocial Approach to Family Life* (Chicago: University of Chicago Press, 1959), p. 261.

[7] Erika Chance, *Families in Treatment* (New York: Basic Books, Inc., Publishers, 1959), p. 156.

bear the weaknesses of each of the others. It is a theory of scapegoating developed not as a tribal phenomenon but as a phenomenon within the family while all members continue to live and interact with the scapegoated member. (50) As a theory it rests upon the assumption of the dynamic unity of the family in its interpersonal transactions. That certain families may need to have one of its members be sick so that the rest may be well indicates the high price that one member may be required to pay for the well-being of others.

A partial confirmation of Garre's formulations about the family and its "ill" member is revealed in the intensive psychiatric evaluation made of lower class families in connection with the Midtown Manhattan Study. (2) The authors of this study found that where infrequent employment at sub-standard wages puts a family in constant peril of disruption and dislocation, the mother assumes the deadly role of disparaging the adequacy of her breadwinner husband. As the child joins her in this grim bout he rejects the father as having a claim to family respect and authority. By this he courts damage not only to the father but to himself since social authority as a beneficient factor in personal development is being rejected along with the father. The disintegrating forces which spread into rejection of school, law and society are but ripples from frightful stones which the overburdened mother casts within the family constellation. The authors of this study are bold to say that society itself by substandard wages and its irresponsibility about the costs of poverty casts the first stone against the lower socio-economic family.

Family treatment. The upshot of this thinking about the family as a psycho-social unit and of personality as an interpersonal phenomenon has come in a variety of approaches to treatment of the family. If the unit of disturbance in living is the family rather than the individual, the unit which should receive psycho-therapeutic help is the family. Martin Grotjahn (64), Nathan Ackerman (58, 59, 65), C. F. Midelfort (57), and Virginia Satir (68), have each written about their work with the family as a unit of disturbed living. In each instance we have a significant break with the individual treatment situation which has prevailed even when parents accompanied "problem" children to clinics.

Even more startling is the breakthrough in family treatment with the most severely disturbed individuals, the schizophrenic. Two psychiatrists, T. Lidz (66) and Don D. Jackson (61, 62, 63), have reported their therapeutic work with the schizophrenic and his family in a variety of recent papers. The individualism of personality theory and of psychotherapeutic treatment is being challenged across a broad spectrum of the helping professions.

Our pastoral interest in this breakthrough which sees and deals with the family as a unit is strong. These newer, fuller understandings of the social nature of the person and this new readiness to deal with the social context of the family as the unit which is to be helped conforms more to the pastor's perception of persons as members of familial units. It also supports through theory and clinical practice the various ways of working with families when disturbances arise in which the pastor already is involved. Previously the pastor called into a family problem had felt out on a limb. All the pastor was able to see in looking over the literature of psychotherapy was that the isolated purity of the clinical interview situation was the proper way to help others. This seemed most remote and untrue to family life as he was called to move around in it and knew it.

Now, he can feel that there are others who have come to see the familial context of individual life. Now, he can find approaches to working with the family as a group which will inform and shape the mainline of pastoral involvement which he already exercises. Now the fact of his pastoral relationship to every member of the family including the youngest child need not be a source of embarrassment as though it were a misfortune of his calling compared to other helping resources. Now he can utilize the peculiar fact of being pastor to all family members as a basis for working with them as a family group whenever problems arise.

CHAPTER FOUR

An APPROACH To FAMILY COUNSELING

The Terms of Family Counseling

The family as a group.   The family as a group is seen by the pastor in family counseling. This includes father, mother and the "difficult" child. It may include other siblings than the "difficult" one, depending on the proximity of ages and the degree of parental pressure being placed on more than one child. Working with the family as a group is a bright change from isolated and repetitive individual appointments. Normally something significant and helpful is accomplished in a *single* session. This too marks a departure from past patterns.

A family problem usually means that a child has become incomprehensible to its own parents. The images which each holds of self and others are disparate rather than congruous. Communication between parents and child is blocked because "who one is talking to" is not the same person as he holds himself to be.

The purpose of family counseling is to open up communication between family members by finding the points of incongruity in the images of self and others and by helping the parents to see the way in which the behavior of the "mysterious child in their midst" is a function of their own expectations and demands. Family counseling helps free a family from its costly preoccupation with its problem and return it to the larger community of the church and world for their role of service there. It helps the family within the congregation to a new readiness to hear the Gospel of God's reconciling work in Jesus Christ as they have participated in a work of human reconciliation offered in testimony to that which God has done.

A single session is usually adequate to accomplish these purposes.

But the single session runs well beyond a single hour. It is divided into a series of four parts:

1. Meeting the family as a group briefly   (2–5 minutes)
2. Speaking with the child alone   (10–20 minutes)
3. Conversation with the parents alone   (15–30 minutes)
4. Meeting with the family as a group   (30–60 minutes)

The time indications are approximate and flexible. They are given to suggest proportions of each part of the session in relation to the others.

The process flow of the session involves two stages. In the first stage the pastor works alone with the child and alone with the parents to find the points of incongruity in images of self and others. (See Chapter Five) In the second stage he works with the family group so that the parents can be helped to see the role of their own images and behavior in creating the mystery in the child. The child may also see his or her own responsibility in the family difficulty at this time. (See Chapter Six)

When does the pastor suggest a single family counseling session to parishioners? *Whenever parishioners indicate that they are having trouble with a child in the family, the child is of school age and you have reason to believe neither parent is "seriously disturbed."* Where there is a seriously disturbed parent, the disruption in family communication may be more a function of inner psychic conflicts than of broken communication between persons. Normally the pastor's own knowledge of the family will be sufficient to guide him in making a judgment of whether there is a seriously disturbed adult or not. Here we find the pastor's diverse relationships with the family are a distinct advantage which he holds over the separated clinician or private practitioner.

If the child is below school age, then the responsibility for any difficulty with the child is quite easily acknowledged as a parental responsibility. The parental appeal most likely will come in the form of a request for help to themselves. Once school age (from five and six on) emerges the parents may protest the mystery is in the child and begin to insist that it is the child who needs to be changed; or at the very least they may protest that they need help in coping with their child. Their own responsibility may be partially owned and partially disowned, or totally disowned. In either case, something is to be done with the child, from the parents point of view. Setting an appointment for a family counseling session meets this request of the parent and involves the parent as well.

Avoiding stigmatization of the child is one of the helpful realities in family counseling. Too often parents encountering difficulties in family living want to locate the problem in the child and hustle *the child* off to a specialist. Most child guidance centers by their very existence implicitly encourage this. Fortunately the change in thinking within these clinics is leading to inclusion of the family in the treatment. If stigmatization is to occur, the parent is to share in it fully. The pastor stands at a point where he can stop some of this stigmatizing of the child as a "problem child" before it snowballs and does its damaging worst through the process of seeking help itself. Through his proximity to the family and the frequency with which he is first consulted when problems arise, the pastor can head off the process of singling out the child as a "problem" by immediate involvement of the parents in a responsible role for the family's well-being or its troubles.

Two Process Flow Stages

(1) *Finding the role incongruities.* A family with a problem is a family of *eccentrics*. With respect to images of self and others each holds, parents and child are off-center. The initial task is to find where the weight of the eccentric pull is located. There is an exploratory responsibility at this stage, first with the child, and then with the parents. The questions of the pastor in conducting this exploratory phase of the session are aimed at finding the present self-understanding or image of self and the present image of the others. It is not depth, analytical exploration. It is exploration in terms of role images. Hess and Handel call the concept of image a "mediating concept. Its reference extends into the personality and out into the interpersonal relationship."[1]

The *mode* of inquiry is one of empathic interest in the world revealed in the images of each person. One reason for seeing the child alone briefly and the parents alone briefly is to convey to each your willingness to see the world of images and perceptions held by each

---

[1] Robert Hess and Gerald Handel, *op. cit.*, p. 6.

as a real world and not a pseudo-world. The fact of conflict between the worlds of the parent and that of the child does not mean one is right and the other is wrong. Each is relating to the other in terms of images held of self and other. The conflict comes because the images lack congruity. Each is off-center in some way. Sensitive openness and warmth of understanding of the present eccentric images is the first requirement as the pastor meets the family counseling session.

Questions of inquiry in this exploration are secondary to the mode of empathic warmth and readiness to think in terms of the world of the other. Within that mode, questions such as these constitute the *form* of the inquiry.

With the child alone:

How do things look to you? Or, what do you think is the problem in your family?
This inquiry should lead to some image of child-self and some image of parents as other than self.

How do you think your parents see you?
This gives the child's view of the parents' child image.
How do you think your parents see themselves?
This gives the child's view of the parents' self-image.

Within a very brief space one catches four images which may be seen diagrammatically in Figures 2 and 3 (pages 80 and 81). The circles above the diagonal lines belong to the child. In Figure 2 they are drawn to suggest congruity of images and ease of interaction between child and parent. In Figure 3 they are drawn to suggest incongruity (the elliptical broken-line images) and the likelihood of turbulence in the interaction. Disturbance in the relationship is suggested by the degree of incongruity between circles I, II, III and IV, existing in the child and corresponding circles i, ii, iii and iv in the parent. Further difficulty can be seen in the incongruity between Child circles I and II, and between III and IV. Similarly within the parent.

The inquiry with the child alone is followed with an inquiry similar in mode and form with the parents alone. The four images in the diagrams belonging to the parent world (the items below the diagonal lines in Figures 2 and 3) are elicited at this time.

The points where agreement exists between any of the four images of the child and the four images of the parent will suggest areas of relative harmony in the relationship. The points where any of the four images of the child and their corresponding images in the parent are at variance will highlight the disharmony in the relationship.

(2) *Facilitating parental insight.* The second stage of the session brings the parents and child (or children) together with the pastor. Now is the time to draw the various images together taking particular note of those places where incongruities have been found. The basic task at first is reportorial. The various images of self and other held by parents and by child have been given to the pastor separately. He now enters into the thick of things. As one writer on family counseling puts it, the counselor is "drawn into the center of the family disturbance . . . into the very center of the whirl-pool."[2]

The report of incongruities leads to the problem of the inner dynamics tying them together. The chief assumption with regard to dynamics is that the mystifying or disturbing element in the child is a function of parental behavior and expectations. The child is fulfilling the terms extended by the parents, but the parents do not see themselves as serving these expectations to the child.

Sometimes simply matching parental role images with the child's role images opens a light. A perspective is given to the parents by their own seeing of the relation between their views and the problems they are complaining about in the child. Such was the case with the Carpenters. They complained that their Tim had become a greater mystery and problem to them just in the past month. When the first grade teacher noted the change in Tim's behavior the parents felt sure something was wrong with Tim.

Mr. and Mrs. Carpenter saw themselves as having to deal with a mysteriously changed child. They also casually reported themselves as intensely troubled over an antagonistic neighbor without seeing any connection at first. The concern with the neighbor had centered on the neighbor's erratic grant of permission to Tim to play in their yard directly across the street. Mrs. Carpenter had developed a phobic concern about the neighbor's house and yard and thus became

---

[2] Nathan Ackerman, "Further Comments on Family Psychotherapy," in Stein, Morris I. ed., *Contemporary Psychotherapies* (New York: The Free Press of Glencoe, 1962), p. 252.

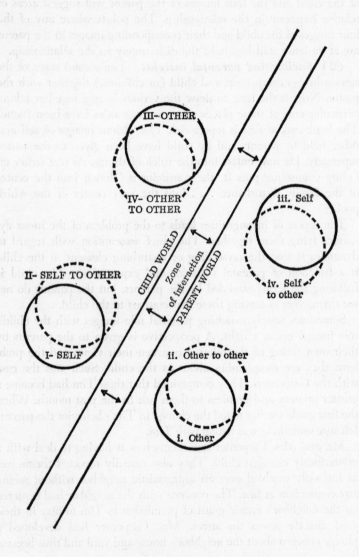

FIGURE 2. A diagrammatic scheme of congruity in the parent-child relation.

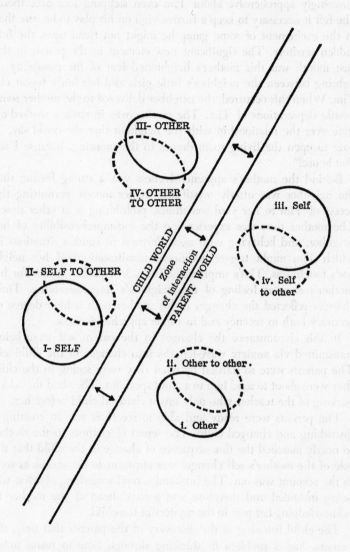

FIGURE 3. A diagrammatic scheme of incongruity in
the parent-child relation.

hoveringly apprehensive about Tim even stepping foot over there. She felt it necessary to keep a furtive vigil on his play to be sure that in the excitement of some game he might not tread upon the forbidden territory. The significant new element in the parent in the past month was this mother's heightened fear of the possibility of fighting between the neighbor's little girls and her burly 6-year old Tim. When this occurred, the neighbor delivered to the mother some hostile deprecations of Tim. The mother was in such a worked-up state over the relationship with the neighbor that she could say, "I hate to open the living room drapes in the morning, because I see *that* house!"

Behind the mother's apprehensiveness was a strong feeling that the neighbor was utterly mystifying in her moods, permitting the access of Tim to her yard sometimes, prohibiting it at other times. The mother thus was experiencing the incomprehensibility of her neighbor, and behaving with new alertness to sudden situations in which Tim might trigger additional manifestations of her neighbor's touchiness. Tim's unpredictability was a perfect match for his mother's anxious feeling of the neighbor's unpredictability. Tim's changes reflected the changes in his mother with a high degree of accuracy both in recency and in vague apprehensiveness.

In this circumstance the changes in the parent self were being transmitted via anxiety wave-lengths into changes in the child-self. The parents were so startled by what they were seeing in the child they were about to send him to a child specialist. They had the added backing of the teacher who only saw a changed child before her.

The parents were ready and able to see their role in creating a disturbing and changed child. The report of changes in the mother so nearly matched the time-sequence of change in the child that the role of the mother's self changes was apparent to her almost as soon as the account was out. The husband sensed something of what was being unfolded and therefore was a step ahead of the mother in acknowledging her part in the mystery of the child.

The child listening to the discovery of the parents that *they*, the parents, had a problem in thinking through how to relate to an erratic neighbor found that *he* was not the big issue after all. To be sure he was in no position to claim understanding of his own behavior, but what 6-year old is? He was not asked to explain his own changes but invited to see his parents were bothered by something other than just his resonating response to their upset.

The pastor stepping into the midst of this family problem feels as though his role is that of defusing explosive materials which if left untouched could continue to accumulate distorting potential.

There had been serious talk of sending *the child* to a psychiatrist because *he* had changed so mysteriously. The upshot of a single session was to move the mystery back from the child through the parents to the parent-neighbor relation. This led to some tentative searching on the parents' part for the anxiousness in the neighbor which was making her so unpredictable and irascible.

A second contribution which the pastor makes to the parents beyond helping them to see the role of their own attitudes and images on the behavior of the child is that of taking the child as objectively sound, reasonable and well-intentioned. Taking the child into conference a few minutes alone right off suggests this to the parents. Then later seeing the pastor in his relationship to the child gives them a glimpse of another adult seeing the child without the distortions of their own emotions.

In another family counseling session the parents of a very bright 9-year old girl were puzzled over what to do with her. Knowing her actual years and their responsibilities as parents, they could not accord the child the greater responsibility for herself which she was seeking. In *his* own conversation with the child the pastor realized that intellectual gifts in abundance were giving to a 9-year old the logic of a mid-adolescent and a sense of responsibility which was truly adult. He decided there was only one convincing way to deal with the sharp incongruity between the child's image of her abilities and the parental doubts regarding these. In the family group conversation in the second stage of the process he consulted the 9-year old daughter's judgment on every problem and "mystery" the parents had presented. Her responses were filled with obvious maturity and judgment. The pastor's response made it clear he felt he could add little, as indeed nothing more mature could be added. It was like talking with another adult if one could forget the slight voice and legs not reaching the ground picture she presented. The parents saw objectively in the dialogues with the pastor the reality of a much older child than they had been willing to believe was the case. Revision of their views of the child in the direction of the child's own appropriate self-judgments were occuring in that very hour as they observed another adult conversing with their child. The father and mother "knew" they were dealing with something other than a 9-year old yet had been unable to make a shift to treating the adult mind in their midst as an adult at such points where judgment and reason —as distinct from emotional needs—were at issue. Seeing another adult speaking with their child in mature conversation without condescension helped this parental change.

Sometimes the parental role in relation to the disturbance in the child is not quickly or easily seen. A hard truth is encountered. This is the case in the family session found in the next two chapters. The interesting matter to observe with regard to gaining parental insight on the parent's part is that first one parent sees the other's part and then the other sees the first one's involvement. Each parent acknowledges the reality of a parental complicity in the child's difficulty by observation of the other parent before drawing the conclusion with regard to self-complicity.

Extra-Session Dynamics

Before the session.   Two additional sets of forces released by family counseling should be noted even though they operate outside of the session. The process of setting a family appointment means that the family must talk over with the child in a very direct way their unhappiness with things as they are. In doing so they indicate something new to the child. The child has no doubt heard their unhappiness many times before, but he or she has heard it with an accusing finger pointed right at him or her. This time the child hears the parents point the finger at themselves as well as himself. Sometimes the child does not believe the parent. The child may suspect the talk about "we" have a problem is just a ruse to get the child to the pastor. However, that the visit is to be with the pastor suggests the child is not being tricked into a situation where all the adults will be lined up against him. On the grounds that the pastor is going to talk things over with the family the child may feel a safety which he could not accord to an unknown adult.

As the parents point the fingers at themselves the child hears—

perhaps for the first time—that the family disturbances are not all his own handiwork. Sometimes the parents have to make very explicit confession of their own frailty and need for a better understanding. The beginnings of a new relationship are inherent in this admission. The seeking of help is to be a family's act in trying to improve matters which belong to the family as a whole. The child and parents are alike in their common responsibility to the family and approach the family counseling session as people who must work together on their common problem. Adversity reaps a reward when it is honestly faced as a common problem before the family ever reaches the appointed hour with the pastor.

After the session. Following the session together the family returns to its own business of living. But there are a number of differences. First of all there is no second appointment set except for the assurance that another one could be made *after three or four months.* (If need arises, they may call at once, of course.) The family is told by this that their life together is their responsibility. At the same time they are assured that the same kind of resource is available again after they have worked a bit on their mutual responsibility of family life.

The session itself has served as an exercise in two processes which are helpful in all interpersonal relations. The first of these is the work of awareness. To become aware of others as they see themselves and to become aware of one's own self perceptions means that a rational pause in the normal exchanges of life has occurred. A momentary reflection about what is going on in myself and what is going on in the other person can lend reasonableness to a situation which has been clouded with emotional generalizations. Both the parents and the child in their separate sessions with the pastor are engaged in this kind of reflective pause. Perhaps it is the first time. It may not be the last. The family counseling session is a training experience in the reconciling work in which they—parents and children—should be engaged whenever disruption and alienation occurs.

The second exercise has been in seeking the reasons *within* rather than without. A disturbed family means that there are disturbed persons doing something to each other. What seems like the other's fault cannot be blandly accepted as exclusively his. The sinister and the alienating powers of life are a part of our own personal being fully as much as anyone else's. The first clue we may get that there is some dismembering force at work in our relation to the family (or to marriage, or to work, etc.) is the perception of behavior in others which we do not want. Further inquiry reveals our own part in that unwanted pattern of behavior. Such an inquiry is practiced during the second stage of the counseling process and it is a helpful training for the future. Seeking the reasons in oneself for disturbances in the interpersonal matrix of the family should take priority over finding these in others.

The shift from looking for reasons in others to looking for reasons in oneself may reverse the vicious cycle. The explanation of why we so frequently find "causes" of interpersonal difficulties in others is that there is something which the other person does which is a responsible act. What we may not see is that it is also a responding action. Thus, our response to a responsible responding action may appear only at the level of holding the other responsible and so the vicious cycle builds. Catching a glimpse of the responding quality of the unwanted action for which another is responsible means we catch a glimpse of something which we are doing. When this happens we may take the steam out of the previously held position that what we do not like is all of the other's own doing. This is a rewarding moment for the pastor in the family counseling session. It does not seem far-fetched to suppose it is not isolated. Rather I assume it is a repeated moment of truth especially for the parents at subsequent times. The fact that family groups rarely take up the offer of a further session after three or four months is the reason for this assumption.

We are ready now to examine this approach to family counseling through the flesh and blood circumstance of a fully recorded session. Chapters Five and Six present a single family session in its verbatim actuality.

CHAPTER FIVE

A FAMILY COUNSELING SESSION—Part I

Finding Role Discrepancies

The first part of a family counseling session is used to establish the role expectancies held by parents and by child. The way in which each looks upon the other as well as upon self is the matrix for their interaction. The disturbance in their life together will be located at those points where major discrepancies occur in the images each holds.

The following family counseling session took place over five years ago. It was arranged following the pastor's attendance at one of the Couples Christian Concern Groups which had been held that evening in the home of Mr. and Mrs. Betterly. They stopped the pastor at their door at the end of the evening saying the two of them felt they were having a problem with their daughter which they would like help on. An appointment was set up on a Saturday about ten days away so that father, mother and daughter could all come together. They agreed to do so.

The Betterlys are active members of a suburban church. They participated in a Christian Concern Group for over four years prior to this session. They are regular in church attendance and active in adult study programs in spring and fall. They are in their early or middle thirties. They have two children, one son Jimmy who is about nine, and the daughter Mary who is nearing eleven. Mr. Betterly works in a graphic arts occupation. Mrs. Betterly had come to the pastor for help on a personal problem about a year a half earlier. At that time the pastor had referred her for a series of counseling talks with a lay woman who had undertaken to exercise a ministry of pastoral counseling as one of her ministries within the congregation. The pastor's relation to the lay counselor was one of training and supervising her in this work. Mrs. Betterly was seen by the lay counselor about a half-dozen times and felt helped by the opportunity this had given her to think about some things which had a bearing on her presenting symptoms.

On the basis of pastoral knowledge of this couple and supervisory knowledge of Mrs. Betterly's counseling earlier, the pastor felt that there was no serious disturbance so localized in either Mr. or Mrs. Betterly as to counterindicate a family session.

Permission to record the session was requested before the recording machine was turned on.[1] This was granted without question. Mrs. Betterly's prior counseling with a lay counselor had already exposed her to the routine use of a recording machine.

1. Meeting the Family Briefly

MOTHER 1:   I . . . ah . . . in fact I saw Mary's teacher yesterday. I had a conference with her. And it's not a new problem, it's the same thing that has, she's had the same problem ever since she's been in school, and, ah, one of the main things is that she hasn't any *self-control* (1)[2] which is something that she needs to work on. And . . . ah . . . we feel that *Mary is very demanding* in attention (2) and . . . ah . . . many times in trying to get attention that she would like to have and the praise that she would like to have many times . . . like all of us . . . she goes about it the wrong way and instead of maybe getting praise for something she's done, she's overstepped someplace and instead she's getting criticism. And

---

[1] Copies of the tape recording of this Family Counseling Session are available to ministers' groups, seminary teachers and interested research people by writing directly to the author at 409 Prospect Street, New Haven, Connecticut, 06511. Copies of this tape recording will be distributed at the cost of $5.00 each. The full recording is at 3¾ ips on both sides of a seven inch reel (1200' long tape).

[2] The material italicized is role descriptive. Each italicized passage is numbered in serial order as it appears. When the same content is repeated later, it still is given the number of the original statement. These statements are tabulated in role sectors for the parents and the child at the end of this chapter.

that's hard. And so we thought maybe you could *help us, help John and I to understand Mary's problem better and help her* (3). *Mary doesn't feel it is a problem* (4) and yet, John and I are looking to the future. We feel that if we can give her help now in learning to handle self-control and sharing with others, which she does, but at the same time she likes to be first and *sometimes she feels left out, I mean that she isn't getting her share* (5). And *we try to give Mary the same share of everything as we do for Jimmy. We try to divide it evenly* (6). Although there are times *when she feels that she isn't getting hers* (6) and I suppose Jimmy feels he isn't always getting his share either. (Pastor: Well . . .) And so this, and the other, there is one other thing and that's the fact that Mary . . . and her teachers have always said *she's a very capable child* (7), a very capable girl . . . *she can do much better work than she is doing.* (8) But she has the attitude that, "Well, why should I work any harder." And this . . . her teachers . . . is something that bothers her teachers because they want her to work to, up to her capacity, if possible, for her own sake; and they, they feel that she definitely can do better than she is doing. But *she doesn't seem to care. She doesn't have this, the drive to do better* (8) And we would like to help Mary so that she does have this *desire to make better grades* and this; not, not that she, ah, not that we want her to give up all of her pleasures and just sit at home and study and nothing else. But perhaps having a little more *self-control* and *working a little harder* (9) at the time allotted for studies, instead of maybe looking around and thinking, "Well, now what am I going to do when this is over, or what will I be doing, say at recess?" If she would *apply herself* (8), which she is capable of doing. When she really puts her mind to something, she does it. (airplane noise overhead) It's a matter of finding the interest (Pastor: O.K. . . .)

FATHER 2:   Let me say one thing first, what we, we're, what we're talking about now is *beyond the normal* (10). That's the thing. I mean this is normal throughout childhood, this type of reaction, but this is *a little bit farther than normal.* (10)

PASTOR 3:   Now . . . let me have some time alone with Mary and then I'd like to spend some time with the two of you and see if we can arrive at something that is helpful . . . about 15 or 20 minutes. (Mrs.: I don't seem to be able to get up the stairs or in and out of chairs this morning.) (parents leave)

2. *With Child Alone*

PASTOR 4:   Well, Mary, I take it they think that there's a problem here and, ah, would like to know if there is some way that they can be of help, I suppose. Some way things could be going differently. Ah, what do you think?

MARY 5:   *I don't think there's a problem* (11).

PASTOR 5:[3]   You don't think there's a problem . . . how do things look to you in terms . . . ?

MARY 6:   Well, *I don't think they're very fair* (12). Because once I spent a whole hour on a drawing and when Daddy came home he said it was awful.

PASTOR 6:   Hmmm. And that's apt to happen quite often . . . is this what you feel? That *you're trying* (13) and you don't even get credit for the amount of trying that you do. Is that it?

MARY 7:   Uh huh.

---

[3] Protocol statement numbering indicates two things: (a) when the number for the pastor matches the preceding statement number, it means the pastor's response is essentially a reflective one. (b) When the number of a pastor statement is new it means the pastoral response is one of inquiry regarding role perceptions rather than reflection of feelings. (See Pastor 4.)

PASTOR 7:   That kind of makes you feel like 'what's the use of trying,' I suppose. How are things, how do you see things in terms of school?

MARY 8:   Well, I don't like school for one reason. The teachers are always so unfair.

PASTOR 8:   They're unfair?

MARY 9:   Because I get, I get a detention, because a kid stabs me in the back and I say 'ouch' and I get a detention.

PASTOR 9:   You're the one that gets caught, the one who gets punished and that's unfair. When they say that you lose your temper, what do they mean by that?

MARY 10:   Well, I just don't think it's fair, and then *I get mad and I start yelling* (14).

PASTOR 10:   I guess you're saying you only yell because it is something . . . something's been provoking, and gotten you into a situation.

MARY 11:   And, *most of the time I do get caught for things that I didn't do* (13). Like I was sitting in my chair and these two boys were talking and I dropped my pencil and when I turned around to get it then she said that I was in a conversation and I got in trouble and so did the other boys. I didn't say one word.

PASTOR 11:   You feel she has it in for you?

MARY 12:   Because last year, Mrs. Kittridge, that was my teacher, didn't like me, see? And I figure that she told the other teachers, that I wasn't a very good student and ever since then I've had trouble.

PASTOR 12:   It's been right from the start of the year? You kind of feel as though you're battling against some pretty tremendous odds here then, huh? (Pause) When they say you're not working as hard as you could and not doing as much as you could in terms of . . .

MARY 13:   . . . because when I get, when I *do my hardest* (13) and then when I get home my Dad says it isn't very nice, he says, 'it looks funny,' then *I don't feel that it's very nice* (crying).

PASTOR 13:   You feel that's just awful unfair, huh? (Mary: 'Thank you' . . . for Kleenex) You feel he's pretty, pretty harsh on you, huh? (Nods) You feel he isn't as harsh on Jimmy? (Nods) So that you really feel that you get picked on, is that it?

MARY 14:   And I do things and Mama says 'they're nice,' and when Jimmy does things she says 'they're wonderful,' and she's so in 'love with all' that . . . (12)

PASTOR 14:   You kind of get to feeling he can't do anything wrong.

MARY 15:   *I just don't think it's very fair* (12). And at Girl Scouts, the other leaders always pay attention to their kids but mother never comes over to me or helps me with anything, she expects me to carry most of the load . . . *it's not very fair* (12).

PASTOR 15:   That is, you lose out with her being a leader, is that it?

MARY 16:   Well, I want her to be the leader, but *if she just paid more attention to me* (17), I'd like it better.

PASTOR 16:   Ummm. You end up being completely left out of it, is that it?

MARY 17:   Yes, and all the other girls' mothers are always helping them and when I ask her to help me she says, 'Well, ask somebody that knows how to do it.' (sobs)

PASTOR 17:   She kinda just says you're on your own, huh? (Pause —27 seconds) Do you have studying to do at home?

MARY 18:   Some times my social studies and stuff, Mommy helps me with.

PASTOR 19:   Do they keep, do they keep after you to do your studying?

MARY 20:   Yeh. I have a choice of doing it before or after dinner and I do it after dinner and Daddy helps me with my arithmetic, because last year I got low grades in it and so this year whenever I make a mistake and I don't understand things, he starts yelling at me. And he says, 'whenever you have problems, always come to me.' So when I come to him if I don't say the right thing, he yells at me. *He wants me to be perfect all the time and it's not easy* (18).

PASTOR 20:   So you come to him because you (un-hmm) need help and then he thinks this is just horrible that you need help. And still he says you're supposed to come to him. (Yeh.) That's kind of . . .

MARY 21:   And he says, 'if you don't hang up your clothes, then, you're going to bed five minutes earlier.' Well, he found one of my old gloves that was in the, in the place where the puppies was, that's where we keep all of our old clothes, and he started yelling at me and I had to go to bed five minutes earlier because it was in there. *I didn't think that was very fair* (12). I'm always finding things of Jimmy's. When I tell Mommy that I found some of his things, she says, 'Let it go until I find it.' Well, when she does, when she does find it all she says is, 'Jimmy, here's your hat.' And Jimmy doesn't have to go to bed earlier. Just me.

PASTOR 21:   The rules don't, don't hold for both of you. Jimmy gets a real break every time. (Un-Hmm) I guess you just kinda feel that you can't please them . . . and give up trying, is that it?

MARY 22:   Uh huh . . . and then when I do try, then Mommy says it's nice and for me to keep trying and then when I try and nothing happens, then *Mom says*

I'm not trying. And *I try my hardest in most of my subjects* (13). And I try and when I don't get good grades, *Mom says I'm lying and that I'm not trying* (19).

PASTOR 22: They don't recognize, they don't know when you're trying, huh?

MARY 23: Yeh. Not only does she say 'I'm not trying,' *but they don't know if I'm trying or not* (21). *I could try my hardest* (13) and *they say I'm not even trying* (19).

PASTOR 23: Um-hm. Kind of they're quick to tell you . . .

MARY 24: . . . *what to do and what not to do* . . . (23)

PASTOR 24: Everything . . . (Pause) well, I guess you feel up against a pretty tough situation, really (um-hm) when both your teachers and your parents are (Mary: . . . against me, it's not easy) not really understanding you . . . it's a real uphill pull.

MARY 25: Uh huh. Then I try sometimes real hard and Daddy says, well why don't I try harder and I can't try harder . . . and it's just awful.

PASTOR 25: You kinda just don't know what to do to please them.

MARY 26: I can't turn to anybody for help because *everybody is against me* (23).

PASTOR 26: Kind of, the people you, you expect to be of help to you (Mary: against me) are not, are not pulling for you at all. (telephone interruption)

PASTOR 27: Sorry for that interruption, (Pause) How do you think your, your Mommy and Daddy look at you. I mean how do you think they see things?

MARY 28: Well, they see things a lot differently than I do . . . *I don't think they care about what happens to me* (24), but what happens to Jimmy is awful . . . and everything is for Jimmy. And the other night my Grandfather promised me that if he shot a deer Mommy would make me something out of it; so now Mommy is going to make Jimmy something when she promised me.

PASTOR 28:   I guess you're saying you see them as caring an awful lot about Jimmy, and just not at all about you.

MARY 29:   Yeh. And when I get up in the morning to go to school at 6:30 and I'm cranky because I didn't get enough rest from the night before and then Mommy is mad at me because I don't want to wear this dress or that dress; and it's just not fun any more (25).

PASTOR 29:   Just the whole day starts wrong.

MARY 30:   (Sobs) Then it stays wrong for the whole day.

PASTOR 30:   What do you think makes them unhappy with you?

MARY 31:   I don't know. But I'm just not *the kind of perfect child that they want* (18) and I can't ever be perfect, because my Dad said so. But I don't know what else I can do now and *they're always telling me to do this and do that; and when I do it, it's to do something else* (22).

PASTOR 31:   Uh huh (Pause) Well, it's quite a struggle.

MARY 32:   With your teacher against you and your parents against you *it's just not easy to hold out any longer* (26). There's nothing you can do.

PASTOR 32:   You're just sunk.

MARY 33:   Yeh . . . *you just sit and wait until they change their minds about you* (27) and they'll take you back in. It's just like being out of the family when they won't help you with anything. It's *not very fair to me* (12), because I'm always the one that gets left out . . . and last night Mama told me—I—I slept the night at my friend's house—and Mama told me that all they were going to do was go out and get a hamburger and come home and then they have my favorite dinner . . . steak and all kinds of stuff.

PASTOR 33:   Kind of, you missed, missed out.

MARY 34:   When they tell you one thing (Pastor: . . . and do something else) and you believe them and then they go and fail you and then when they tell you to always believe your parents you just can't because *they never do what they tell you they're going to do* (28).

PASTOR 34:   You just can't be sure of them.

MARY 35:   Yes. Mom says, 'you believe all the kids on the block except your parents.' Well, what else am I supposed to do? *My parents tell me one thing and then they don't do it* (28).

PASTOR 35:   Uh huh. Well, I guess this helps me see what's happening for you and now I would like to talk to your mother and father for a little bit and then I'd like to talk with the two of you together, the three of you together, OK?

MARY 36:   OK (Child leaves; parents return).

3. With Parents Alone

PASTOR 36:   I guess I'd like a chance with the two of you now to get a picture of how you see Mary—if you want to elaborate in any way from what you were saying—that basically, she is *not working up to her ability* (7) and some worries about what this means and you have reports of temper, *loss of temper* (1) at school and so on . . .

FATHER 37:   I think it goes deeper than that, Pastor. We've, Ann and I, if we have laid awake at nights past our regular bedtime hours for hours into the night discussing this thing once, we have done it, I don't know how many times. And the funny thing about it is we have done this for almost 11 years. Mary as a baby showed, was very indifferent about being loved; and you try to pick her up and hold her and she just wouldn't; she wanted to get down. You try to love her up or anything—she wanted no part of it. *Now . . . she just can't seem to get enough of it* (2). Ah . . . we try to love her, and we do love her, of course we love her, but it's just that she doesn't seem to have a—that we can't give her enough. There is, is not enough love in this world for her and as a result, as Ann says, *she is constantly fighting for attention, for praise, and everything else* (2), . . . over and beyond her brother and her mother and her father and everyone else. *We don't know whether it's extreme self-centered selfishness, or whether it's insecurity or what this basic thing is* (3). And it's all these things together which cause, I'm sure, this trouble in school. I mean, this is just not lack of initiative in school, nor is it lack of self-control. I think it all comes down to these other things that causes this. See . . .

PASTOR 37:   You're kind of saying there's a, there's a basic demanding here on her part that is, that presses you, presses you to the wall really!

FATHER 38:   Really, it does and it exasperates you. You want to express your love but, and at the same time you know that if you go that far (gestures) you're going to get drawn this much farther (gestures) and finally you, you *are* at the wall. And Ann and I are both only children. (Sigh) Frankly, *we're probably not the best parents* (29) . . . let's put it this way, we've never been educated to be the best parents. This is something that either comes normal or doesn't come normal. We've done everything that we think we can do and should do. And I think *primarily the problem is with us* (A) of knowing how to handle her and how to care for her.

MOTHER 39:   And yet we've got two children, not one.

FATHER 40:   The other one is exactly the opposite.

MOTHER 41:   She would have been a perfect only child, because she would have received all of the attention then.

FATHER 42:   She has a terrific *adult yearning* (30) and as I say, again, I'm fully aware of other children, I mean, when I say the things I say, this probably sounds normal for any child, but *she seems to want to go beyond this* (10). For example, we've always heard in this matter of sex that they'll ask a question and then drop it. But not her. It goes on and on and on. In the matter of dating, or anything like that, now she wants this type of thing and yet she's not really old enough to have the responsibility that goes with it. I mean, some girls mature early and you don't mind, because they have the responsibility and the sense of reality to go ahead on some things like that, but not with Mary. She's still . . . not even 11 yet, but yet she wants these older type things. She's crazy about wearing lipstick . . . and will get into it at every advantage. Ahm. Even to the extent where we ignored it at first, figuring it would pass, but this doesn't pass. She wants to sample alcohol or smoke cigarettes . . . and things like this, that to me it looks like she wants to be grown up ahead of time, but . . . and this is the thing that bothers us for the future . . . that we, we, *neither one of us are coped for a wild teenager* (31) . . . and we're trying to get at this thing now . . . because . . .

PASTOR 42:   Really, because of her curiosities at this point, you really have fears for . . .

FATHER 42:   Trouble later on . . .

PASTOR 42:   . . . how far she would move into things which I suppose you would expect most kids to have some reticence about.

FATHER 43:   That's the thing Ann can tell you about. She doesn't seem to have any . . . how did you phrase it, last night?

MOTHER 44:   Well, I was telling John that *her timing is very poor* (32). She's always *very irritated at me* (33). I happen to have Mary's Scout troop and the other day she was telling me that . . . (Mother explains an incident at a scout meeting which exhibited a lack of tactfulness on the child's part regarding the mother's showing slip.)

FATHER 45:   *She's extremely frank* (32).

MOTHER 46:   Yes, she is . . . if she wants to know something . . . and she's been this way ever since, she's been . . . 'what's this? what's that?' Never, she could never decide whether this is something she should come up with (whispers) 'what do you think?' or 'who is that?' or 'tell me about this.' But when it goes through her mind, she's out with it. It doesn't make any difference where you are or what it's about. If she wants to know, she will not wait. (Mother explains another incident on a bus which embarrassed the mother because the child inquired in a loud whisper about a man's deformed ear.) *She resents Jimmy* (5), has ever since he's been here . . . and yet he doesn't resent her. If he does, his is very mild. He's always had Mary with him. He always thinks of her. (The mother now explains Jimmy's solicitude for his sister and Mary's prevailing resentment of Jimmy. She notes, with appreciation, one exception in the past week where Mary stood up for Jimmy when parents were disciplining him. Mother goes

on to document her not pushing Jimmy off on Mary
as a sitter.) So the feeling of resentment of him
does not come from that. *It's the sharing of attention* (5).

PASTOR 46:   I guess you're saying, you tried to be lenient on her.

MOTHER 47:   Exceptionally so . . . yes. I, I have taken him with
me when really she could, she could have looked
after him and yet, her, she, she doesn't really . . .

FATHER 48:   *She never really understands how much attention
she is getting* (34).

MOTHER 49:   And she, she really *can't determine right from wrong*
(35). Last Saturday, John and I had to run into the
lumber yard and we were gone a little bit longer than
I thought we would be, but the children were all
right. It was in an hour close to dinner time . . .
where much of this time they could be watching television and shouldn't be into any trouble . . . and
we told them that, and came back . . . and,

FATHER 50:   . . . we live in a wood house, you know . . .

MOTHER 51:   Mary had made a dessert, which is fine. She decided
she wanted to make a dessert. That was fine. But they
built a fire in the fireplace! . . . And this is one
thing that we had pointed out to the children, as
John said, we live in a wood house, and we have to
be extremely careful. And when a fire is built,
either John or myself is there. Now occasionally we
let one of the children do it, but it is supervised.
And of course, we were just, well, it's, it's a horrible
feeling and you think, my gosh . . . I could have
come home and both of my children might have
been laying here burned to death—(telephone interruption).

MOTHER 52:   And she was extremely upset because she thought she
had done something so nice for us. And, and, it was

too bad that we had to, to more or less, bawl her out for doing this, because we don't dare let these children light a fire while we're gone. If a spark should . . . (both talking) . . . in their messing with the fire . . . Not in our house. You just cannot do it.

FATHER 53:   It was *beyond the normal* (10). And its not that we hadn't explained this, we had done this . . . I won't let either one of them play with matches unless I am there, because there's cork on the floor and it's wood walls and drapes and everything . . . and wham!

MOTHER 54:   And she said, 'Well Jimmy wanted to build a fire.' And that was all right. But we said to her well you should have said, 'Now Jimmy you know we cannot build a fire when Mother and Daddy are not here.' But the idea—one thought of it, and the other . . . 'oh boy, that would be fun . . . have a fire going when Mother and Daddy come home.' But she is 11, and I feel that she is of the age where *she should be able to say to herself, 'Well, now is this something that is all right for us to do?'* (35). We know other children of 11 that are quite capable of this and yet I know you should not compare your child with some, some other child. But this is, is where Mary wanting to do something (Fa. . . . and knowing you shouldn't) being nice, doing something special so that you would be pleased when you come home and yet her decision on what to do is so wrong. If she had just made the dessert that would have been perfect, you see. But she had to go one step farther and build the fire and of course the whole thing was torn down and *she was quite upset over the fact that she had tried to do something nice and we didn't appreciate it* (36). And it wasn't that we didn't appreciate the thought, but it was that that was wrong in our house for she and Jimmy to build a fire. Now this is, this is Mary. Jimmy and the rest of us can work around a bucket of paint all day and not a drop is spilled and no one gets it on them. Mary could have been gone all day and walked in at 5 o'clock and the bucket of paint is still there, and before you know it, it's either spilled, it's down the front of her, or it's on something. Now, how it happens, I don't know. But, this is Mary, along with *her striving for the attention* (2) and love that she feels she is not getting.

PASTOR 54: I guess I hear you saying she does all sorts of exasperating things, that is, she'll find the exasperating thing to do.

MOTHER 55: Yes. I don't know how to, and I don't know how she finds them to do myself. And yet, there are some times when she is very, very good about things . . . (Fa. : She's very sweet, ah . . .) she'll say, 'well, no,' she can't do this. Now there are some times when she knows that she can't do it. Well, this fireplace business . . . it can probably come up a hundred times from now and I don't imagine she'll ever light another fire unless she's either asked and some things she knows, boy, when she knows she's not supposed to do it, she won't budge. (airplane noise in background) . . . But when it comes to her making a decision in the very beginning *'Is this right or is this wrong?'* (35) . . . I don't know whether inside she thinks 'I shouldn't do it, but on the other hand, it would be so nice to do it,' you see? *This, I don't understand* (37). And yet, she is a *bright child* (7). Her teachers tell us that she is.

PASTOR 55: That is, I guess you're saying you don't know *how* she arrives at these actions on her own . . .

MOTHER 56: No, I don't.

PASTOR 56: . . . in this sense you're saying *she just mystifies you* (37).

MOTHER 57:   Yes. And *she is devilish* (38). There are times when it just pops out all over her and she's full of life. She loves people, and . . .

FATHER 58:   There's one other insight on this. I don't know whether this has any bearing on it or not. But Mary seems to be an individual, there are quite a few of them, I guess, I didn't realize there were. But she's *extremely sensitive, extremely sensitive to pain* (39) in any sort of a way. Now she is almost a hypochondriac. (Father gives illustrations of the child's hypersensitivity to pain.)

MOTHER 59:   And this is coming back to *her thinking she doesn't get enough love* (40).

FATHER 60:   She doesn't seem to realize that other people feel pain, and yet, in her own mind she senses pain terribly. (The father now documents the child's inverse low sensitivity to pain she may inflict on others. A school incident is related.)

PASTOR 63:   It seems as if you're saying, you find her unreasonable.

MOTHER 64:   Yes . . . John was telling you about pain and that. (Mother now related the experience of Mary during an eye test during which the daughter complained greatly about the discomfort. Jimmy made no murmer in same situation.)

FATHER 65:   Well, she expects life to be a complete bowl of cherries with sugar and cream right there no hardships whatsoever. That nothing in life should irritate her or rub her or anything else and . . . life just ain't this way . . . and I want to get her ready for it and, frankly, I think it's probably us that needs the advice. How do we go about this, that, that life is just not a bowl of cherries, that there are other individuals' desires and things that have to be reckoned with and that she has to be a team in society, and that there are bound to be irritations and everything? But this has no effect.

PASTOR 66: How do you see her picture of herself? How, what do you think she thinks of herself?

FATHER 67: *She doesn't think she's good enough* (41) . . . I don't think . . .

(The pastor presses the inquiry for specifics.)

MOTHER 77: Inferior. *Maybe we have set her standards too high* (B). Unfortunately, John, John and I do have, I feel *rather high standards* in work that we do (42). When John does any carpentry around the house he wants it to be right. He doesn't like a sloppy joint. He doesn't want to mitre something together and have a crack in it . . . he wants it to fit. And I like to sew and I *constantly strive for perfection* (42). That's as much a phobia with me as, as whatever is bothering Mary. Because, because I want it to be right . . . I want it to look right, that whatever it is, I want it to be the right color and everything else . . . that's something that's in me, and *perhaps we have made our standards too high for Mary* (B). This I don't know. And when she says she can't attain them, then she has taken the attitude of, well, as long as I can do something and get by with it, then *why strive* any higher. Her teacher says '. . . she hands in . . . her writing is terrible, she says *she doesn't try* (8). Her English is very poor . . . she says, she can do better.'

FATHER 78: And yet she had a vocabulary of a 6-year old when she was two almost. (Mo. : . . . three)

PASTOR 78: You are saying that you see her as feeling not, as though she doesn't measure up, and see yourselves as having held perhaps high standards for her, perhaps believing that she has high ability. And, I guess you are saying by that, that you feel that you have wanted her to measure up, have wanted her to come up to some . . .

FATHER 79: Well, to her own range, the one that she sets for herself. She loves plays and she loves acting, and she likes all these sort of things. But even those things that she loves, she will n . . . well, piano music, she loves music. She sings. She can memorize a song that fast. (snaps fingers) She can hear a melody and she can go down and play it on the piano (7). As much as she likes this, *she will not strive to do anything with it* (8), other than an occasional thing. We give, we give her piano lessons. She begged for piano lessons. That's all we heard about . . . We went out and bought a piano, gave her piano lessons. As soon as she got this, she didn't want to go any farther with it (43). She will get something on her mind that she wants . . . a she wanted . . . what do you call those little animals (Mo.: which one?) . . . Which one? yeah. The guinea pig—like . . . yes, she wanted a guinea pig . . . that's all we heard around the house . . . a guinea pig . . . a guinea pig. So we got it . . . and in two days . . .

MOTHER 80: Well she took her own money . . . we finally told her she could have it (Fa.: If she earned it, if she earned it.) . . . if she would earn the money. And so she finally scrounged around until she found a silver dollar that had been given to her and some other money and finally her allowance sorta mounted up and she finally managed to save the two dollars . . .

FATHER 81: She bought the guinea pig, and I and . . . she and I made a cage for it together and I figured if she worked on the cage with me and help me with the thing which she wanted to, this would build all this thing together . . . Two days later, (snaps fingers) bang. The guinea pig sat. And then nothing to do with it. Except maybe three minutes a day attention, that was it.

MOTHER 82:   She might take it out of the cage and play with it a little bit . . .

FATHER 83:   Then put it away . . . this tremendous *desire that was there was gone as soon as she had what she wanted* (43).

PASTOR 83:   I guess I hear you saying that you see her as feeling inadequate within herself and yet you also see her as not pushing herself.

FATHER 84:   No . . . (Mo.: she won't . . .) She don't want any responsibility or work connected with what she wants . . .

PASTOR 84:   You feel that she, what, that she sees herself as wanting things and not wanting to do anything about them.

MOTHER 85:   And *John is an excellent father* (44), really, to his children.

FATHER 86:   Well, I don't know if I am, but . . .

MOTHER 87:   He takes time out to help them build this or help them to build that. Christmas Day he spends all day on their toys with them, helping them to figure out this, helping them to figure out that and I think there are few fathers that take the time with their children that John has. My dad traveled all the time, he certainly didn't. John's Dad never did it for him. But the children can, will never be able to say that their Daddy didn't sit down and help them, because if they want to build something, by golly, John's got the nails for them and the hammers and he helps them to figure out how to do it and then, of course, he expects them at some point to take over.

PASTOR 88:   How do you think she looks at you? Sees you?

FATHER 89:   I don't know.

MOTHER 90: This is, this is probably one of the greatest things that baffles us . . . baffled both of us.

FATHER 91: Lord knows we love her or we wouldn't even be here.

PASTOR 92: How do you think she sees you?

FATHER 93: I don't know.

MOTHER 94: I would say as a *very strict mother* and *probably as one that's not too understanding* (45).

FATHER 95: She's apt to complain about *us being unfair* (46).

MOTHER 96: I remember when she was very little . . . (mimicking a little child) 'you don't love me any more or you wouldn't make me do this.' And I keep saying to Mary, 'If I didn't love you I wouldn't make you do this. I would just let you go, but I do love you and I want you to do this because it is necessary for you to learn it,' or whatever it might happen to be. But *she thinks we are extremely hard on her.*

PASTOR 96: Strict and unfair.

MOTHER 97: Yes. And what else she thinks, I don't know . . . but those two things, I know that she feels that way. *She's unhappy* (Fa.: Yes, she is) And her teacher says that she's unhappy.

FATHER 98: She's an extreme extrovert . . . (48)

MOTHER 99: We can punish her by making her stay in her bedroom. (Fa.: Yeah) Because she's got books, dolls, paint sets (Fa.: Everything) She can't find one thing to do in her bedroom . . . (She details this point further.)

FATHER 100: She's got, just got to be with people all the time, whether it's with adults or with children, or what . . . (He details this point.)

MOTHER 101: And she wasn't left when she was little . . . (Fa.: No, no) never.

FATHER 102: Because Ann and I are just not the gadding kind. I'm home all the time, so is Ann . . . I mean by that our social activities have never . . . been one that we're in a social world, where we might neglect her and give her to somebody else all of the time because we just don't.

MOTHER 103: And we certainly didn't then because we couldn't afford to when she was little, to go out. Maybe we would go out once a month and that was, that was something if we even did that.

PASTOR 104: Well . . . I think it might be helpful then to spend some time now with the three of you to see if I can in a sense play back to you these various pictures each of you hold of the other and the points where the difficulty comes. I think it would be well to do it with her here, because . . . I think this . . .

MOTHER 105: Do you feel that she will understand this?

PASTOR 106: Oh, yes.

MOTHER 107: She was exceedingly upset over the fact that we were bringing her here today. She was very angry with me. Didn't think it was right at all. She didn't want to come. And I talked to her at great length about it and finally I said to her, 'Well, will you please come just for me?' I said, 'Not for yourself,' but I said, 'I want you to do it for me.' I said, 'I feel there are things I should be doing for you and understanding about you and I don't.' And I said, 'I never had any brothers or sisters and my experience with children has been very small,' and I said, 'I feel the only way I can understand you and children of your age will be to come here today.'

PASTOR 108: What did she say to that?

MOTHER 109: She still didn't want to come. And I said, 'Well, you've just got to, we have made the appointment and Mr. Pastor is going to take his time this morning to see us, and I said 'it would not be fair for us to call him up now and ask him to break the appointment.'

PASTOR 110:   Well, I think it would be very beneficial, more beneficial with the three of you, than, than just to speak to the two of you alone or back to her alone.

MOTHER 111:   Well, now I have one other question to ask. Will you have some constructive suggestions to make on things that we should do or can do to help Mary?

PASTOR 112:   Well, that's what I am going to do now. (Mo.: Yes, well) . . . not in suggestion form, but let you see what you are dealing with in each other and in yourselves.

MOTHER 113:   Well, but I feel that unless we have some very concrete suggestions made . . . John and I have been struggling with this problem now for quite some time and apparently we haven't been able to come to any good solution and I feel that you could probably say, now, 'Well, this is maybe a place where you could do this . . . or you could try this. And . . . ah . . . I'm not speaking for John, I'm speaking for myself because I feel that *I'm very blind* and there are things that are evident that I should be able to recognize and I don't. *My own personality is involved in* this thing too, (C) and perhaps I'm stubborn and just won't give up and say, 'Well, this is it, let's do something about it.' And even if I did know that something should be done, I wouldn't know just where to turn. So that's why I feel we need something where we definitely feel, 'Well, we're going to try this.' (jet in background) . . . I work much better with a pattern.

A SUMMARY OF SELF-OTHER IMAGES

The tabular summary of the four self-other images offered below quickly points to the areas of primary tension and conflict. Item numbers assigned in this summary *before* the statements appear in the preceding text in parentheses following the statement.

These ascending item numbers indicate their order of appearance in the counseling session. The numbers in parentheses following each statement refers to the counseling session's numerical order of protocol statements.

The italicized item represents the point of direct contradiction between the testimony of the child and the parent. Blank space in the parallel column indicates possible areas of lop-sidedness.

The Child	*The Parents*
(I) Self	(i) Other
14. When I get mad I start yelling. (10)	1. She hasn't any self-control. (1, 36)
17. (I wish she) paid attention to me. (16)	2. Mary is very demanding in attention (1) (And love). (She) just can't seem to get enough of it. (37)
15. I get caught for things I didn't do. (11)	5. She feels she isn't getting her fair share, (1) (and resents a brother who does). (46)
	7. She's a very capable child. (1)
13. *I do my hardest.* (6, 7, 13, 22, 23)	8. She can do much better. (1) She doesn't apply herself. (1, 36, 77)
23. Everybody's against me. (26)	10. (She's) beyond the normal. (2, 42)
	30. A terrific adult yearning. (42)
	32. Her timing is very poor. (44) Extremely frank. (45) (Not tactful)
	35. (Poor judgment) Is this right or is it wrong? (49) (55)

26. It's just not easy to hold out any longer.   (32)
11. I don't think there's a problem.   (5)
25. It's just not fun anymore.   (29)
27. You just sit and wait until they change their minds about you.

38. She is devilish. (57)
39. She is extremely sensitive to pain. (58)
43. (No follow through). (79)
47. She's unhappy. (97)
48. She's an extreme extrovert. (98)

(II) Self to other

(See 11 above)

24. I don't think they care what happens to me.   (28)

19. Mom says I'm not trying.   (22, 23)
20. Mom says I'm lazy. (22)
21. They don't know if I'm trying or not.

(ii) Other to other

4. Mary doesn't feel it is a problem. (1)
40. (She thinks) she doesn't get enough love. (59)
41. She doesn't think she's good enough. (67)

See 8 above

See 8 above

(III) Other

12. I don't think they're very fair. (6, 14, 15, 21, 33)

22. (They tell you) what to do and what not to do.   (24, 31)

(iii) Self

3. (We) need help to understand Mary's problem. (1, 37)
6. We try to give Mary the same share of everything we do for Jimmy. (1)
9. (We want our child) to work a little harder. (1)

(III) Other

28. They never do what they tell you they're going to do. (34, 35)

18. He wants me to be perfect all the time and it's not easy. (20, 31)

16. I don't feel it's very nice (of him to depreciate what I do). (13)

(IV) Other to other

(See 17)

(See 24)

(See 20)

(See 12)

(iii) Self

29. We're probably not the best of parents. (38)

31. Neither one of us are coped for a wild teenager. (41)

37. I don't understand (Mary's lack of judgment. (55, 56) I strive for perfection.

42. John and I do have I feel rather high standards. (77)

44. John is an excellent father. (85)

(iv) Self to other

33. She's always very irritated with me. (44)

34. (She doesn't understand how much attention she is getting. (48)

36. (She) tried to do something nice and we didn't appreciate it. (54)

45. A very strict mother and probably one that's not too understanding. (94)

45. Unfair (parents). (95)

The most discordant note in the above is the discrepancy between the child's self-image of "trying" and "trying her hardest" and the parental assertion that the child is not trying to do what she is capable of doing. The parents see and are distressed about apathy in the child. The problem is to help them to see in what way their own behavior and expectations contribute to the distressing signs of apathy which the child presents to them. Underneath, we already have the child's image as being something quite different than not trying. Yet, while she has presented herself as "trying her hardest," she also confirms some of the parental perception of having given up and ceased to try (see Pastor 21). She says she has to "wait until they change their minds about you" and "take you back in the family." (Mary 33). Our task in the balance of the session is to help them do this.

CHAPTER SIX

A FAMILY COUNSELING SESSION—Part II

Facilitating Family Understanding

The problem which this family faces at this point is a typical middle-class family problem. The pressures for success through the early achievement of children are strong. Parents need to be assured of their own social worth. The child's success is one means at their disposal. When parents believe that their child is superior and gifted, fuel is added to the flames. Several comments by the parents in the first hour were of this kind. They reported Mary had a vocabulary of a 6-year old at age two (corrected to three by a note of realism in the mother). There is obvious parental satisfaction in Mary's musical gifts.

The Protestant ethic of diligent effort is also present in the parents. Every day in every way the child is supposed to get a little better by working hard and applying herself. The parental role is that of pushing, prodding and goading the child to better accomplishments. They see themselves as the goal setters.

In the process something goes sour. The child seemingly gives up. The parents think they must push all the harder. The child responds less favorably and more pressure is needed. A vicious cycle is in process. The key to reversal of the vicious cycle is in helping the parents see themselves as contributing to its spiral effects. Three statements in the first hour suggest that the parents are faintly aware of some responsibility for the adverse responses they are getting from their daughter. In the text they were italicized and labeled (A), (B) and (C).

A. Primarily the problem is with us. (38), (65) (By the father.)
B. Maybe we've set her standards too high. (77) (By the mother.)
C. My own personality is involved in this thing too and perhaps I am stubborn. (113) (By the mother.)

Additional data of their own sense of self-involvement and responsibility is the readiness to acknowledge their lack of understanding about children and about what they may be doing as parents to their older child.

As the fourth part of this session begins there is a long statement by the pastor made to the family group—parents and child. In this statement, the pastor tries to indicate both for the child's understanding and for the parents, what the effects of the discrepant role expectations are. The parents are perceived by the child as unfair and are themselves unaware of the child's efforts to please. Consequently the child has given up on the parents—hence her apathetic response. The pastor's endeavor is to help the parents see their prior part in evoking the child's apathy by their blindness to her efforts and their continual setting of higher goals without pausing to give due appreciation to what she has tried to do. We pick up the verbatim record as the pastor seeks to relate the parental role to the child's "not trying."

PASTOR 114:   . . . I get a real sense of Mary's feeling that the cards are all stacked against her. That if she tries, she isn't going to be good enough to please. And so, she's going to be criticized for what she accomplishes. If she doesn't try, she's going to be criticized for not having tried and so she can't win either way. So I kind of think that she's decided that she's lost so it doesn't matter what she does. That is, that if the only thing you're going to get is disapproval or rejection or criticism, why, then it doesn't make any difference what you do. I get the feeling that maybe this is something that she has come to think of was the way to handle herself both at home and at school. It's a kind of 'what's the use?' feeling.

Does it look that way to you, Mary? (Mary nods her head.) I sense you are kind of waiting, Mary, waiting to see if they will change—if they will appreciate something you do, or if they will appreciate you're trying to do things. And you see yourself as making lots of efforts in trying. But, then, but then the additional, the difficulty that's there is, that if you're waiting for them to change and expecting them not to change, just be the same old people, it's kind of hard to get the situation any better on that basis. . . . (To the parents:) Waiting for you to change without expecting you ever to change. She's really expecting you, two things of you, both to be just the same all the time and some day to be different.

MOTHER 115: To wake up and find everything different.

PASTOR 116: Yeh . . . and so this, this just could perpetuate in an inevitable bind for her, for you.

MOTHER 117: May I, may I say something here? I think John and I try in many ways to please Mary and yet we have the feeling that we are not pleasing Mary. If we get her something or John brings home something, or we go some place sort of special, 'It's nice, but . . .', 'It's pretty, but . . .' . And I have gotten to the place that when I give Mary something as a gift, I am wondering what's going to be the 'but' this time. 'It's nice, but it should have been a different color,' or 'it should have had a little something here.' And John and I almost feel defeated before we start. We want to give her something that we know will please her and yet we know for some reason or another it's not going to completely please her. And so . . .

PASTOR 117: I get the feeling that what you are saying is that what you hold within your own self are the same attitudes . . .

MOTHER 118: . . . that she has, yes.

PASTOR 118: . . . that she has, that you want to please her, but you don't think that anything will please her.

MOTHER 119: It's always going to be this, 'It's nice, but' or 'It was a good movie, but' . . .

PASTOR 119:   There's something wrong with it.

MOTHER 120:   Yes, so you see she feels that she is waiting for us to change, and yet she knows we won't. And we are trying to do for her and yet we know she is not going to be satisfied.

PASTOR 120:   Umhmm, you're both caught in the same kind of bind, of trying to make a clean start or do something differently to the good, but expecting that this isn't going to work either.

MOTHER 121:   Very dubious, yes . . . 'nothing else has, why will this?'

The mother sees the point the pastor has made about the child's simultaneous and conflictual trying and giving up. She sees it as the same attitudes within herself and the father. Both are involved in efforts to please the other and pessimism regarding the outcome. At this point the father reassures the child that their coming for help is not disciplinary toward her but seeking help in understanding for themselves. The pastor then attempts a further interpretation regarding the parent's role in the child's apathy. Their high level of aspiration and expectation for the child contributes to the child's continual encounter with parental dissatisfaction.

PASTOR 123:   . . . I think there is another factor that I would like to see if I can get a hold of in terms of what maybe the two of you may be doing that perpetuates the difficulty with Mary. I think you have some appreciation of this kind of thing I have just been saying about what Mary encounters, namely, that she's kind of given up. (Mo.: 'What's the use?') Her best efforts are not seen as good enough whatever they are and so there's no winning. She doesn't try at all, because she hasn't tried. She is beaten either way. She's kind of given up and I think you sense she's given up by your feeling that she feels as though she can't, perhaps can't please, or can't do, can't come up to expectations. (See parental statements 67 and 77 in first hour.) I think this points directly then to what kind of expectation level you are holding within yourselves. If you realize that there's a pretty realistic or strong level of feeling within Mary of 'I can't' or 'what's the use?' and you still go on expecting 'you can' and 'you better,' then this isn't taking account of Mary where she really is; and can only help but keep her in the position of feeling 'I can't' and 'there is no use.' So that you know something that should lead you to feel considerably differently about every situation with her than you actually do; and out of concerns that you put in terms of 'but you know that she's got more ability' or objectively, 'it could be different,' out of those concerns—which are quite external and objective—you keep the pressure high. But out of an appreciation of where she is within yourselves, you know this is wrong.

MOTHER 124:   But we know that she can do better because we have seen her do it. That's what we have to base our standard by.

The mother resists the interpretation of parental responsibility for the child's apathy through over-expectation. The pastor presses the distinction between objective ability and the child's subjective appraisal. The father sees the point and the mother concedes it at 132.

PASTOR 125:   That's quite apart from her though.

MOTHER 126:   Yes . . . but I say that's one of the reasons we hold the standards high because we have seen past performance and know that she is capable although she does not *feel* that she is.

PASTOR 127:   This is, much more important, you see, (Mother: Yes) than whether she can or can't. If she feels that she can't, why then it wouldn't matter if she had the ability of Michelangelo; you would never get up on the scaffold to put something on the ceiling if you felt you couldn't. So that the only place that you can really effectively meet her is where she is in her own feelings, not in terms of where she should be or where she could be.

MOTHER 128: Well, the only thing I was pointing out was that we hadn't just jumped to this high level of expectation of Mary. (talking together) It wasn't done . . .

FATHER 129: No, but what the pastor is saying is regardless of the level, this is the level at which she is.

MOTHER 130: Yes, what I'm saying, we didn't just arrive at this level, just out of our own thoughts. We arrived at it from past experience, and that's why we had set the goal this high.

PASTOR 131: But somehow or other the handling of them . . .

MOTHER 132: . . . has been wrong . . .

PASTOR 133: . . . has been such as to make it impossible now for you to set any. (Father: Umhm.)

The counselor now sets in parallel the discordant expectations each holds with regard to the other, indicating the discord is in the kind of expectations inside each, rather than just in the objective encounter. A series of see-saws occurs with the father and mother alternately seeing and not-seeing the point about overly high standard setting.

PASTOR 133: So that I think each of you has your own fundamental problem with the other. Where in some ways Mary feels that she is trying and wants to be good, but she also feels it's useless and in this sense, she's given up trying. You know what I mean by saying that, Mary? In other words, you say, 'I'm trying' and yet you feel 'what's the use of trying?' And that's a tough spot to be in. But for your parents, I sense them saying they know you feel as though you're having a tough time pleasing them and yet they still want you to be a perfect little girl. And that's hard for them to realize that these are two different things that they are expecting. Just as it is hard for you to realize that you both are trying and have given up trying. You feel it's useless to try. So I think that this is probably the level at which you have to help each other. It's the deepest inner struggle each of you are having within yourself. It's a struggle inside yourself which relates to the other, but it's a struggle inside yourself.

Now the father resists the interpretation while the mother tries to understand:

FATHER 134:   Well, the question I have is—we have a family, four, and we have tried to be fair, but in effect what you are saying is that this is the level that we should understand Mary and come down to this level, but what happens to the rest of the family—in this give in?

PASTOR 135:   Well, it isn't so much giving in as acknowledging that in addition to pure ability, there is her accumulated appraisal of that ability within herself, which has come out in a highly 'I can't' negative form. So that any time you are looking to Mary, for doing this or doing that you have to look to her both as one who is capable but who doesn't now feel that way about herself. So that it isn't as though you are giving in, you are acknowledging there is something there more than just sheer crude motor power and intellectual capacity. There is, there is a girl with her talents plus her feelings about those talents which have accumulated in a way that are detrimental to her use of them.

MOTHER 136:   Is this the reason why she doesn't want to be bothered to further anything? I mean, when she likes something and you get her something to do along that line and because it means work and time on her part she is rejecting it, when we are hoping that this will be the one thing that she will sort of take an interest in and work at it and we would be glad to help her.

PASTOR 137: I would imagine that what you are encountering is initial enthusiasm, yes, but a fundamental failure to follow through growing out of the fact that 'I can't please them anyway.'

Now the mother protests her good intentions and the counselor resists these on behalf of the child:

MOTHER 138: How are we going to make her understand that all that we ask . . . I mean, all that we are hoping for is that she will try to follow through and we will be so pleased and be so willing to help her?

PASTOR 139: Well, what I am saying is that she's not convinced of that.

MOTHER 140: Well, then the question is, how will we convince her? How can she see it?

PASTOR 141: I think you have to accept that this is the way she feels.

MOTHER 142: Are we to sit down and work with her on a project until it is completely done? even though . . .

PASTOR 143: For instance, just take piano playing. Now Mary may not know why she has given up that. Do you know, Mary, why you have given up piano playing? (Shakes her head negatively.)

MOTHER 144: (Speaking to Mary.) Well, yes you do. You didn't want to practice, did you?

PASTOR 145: Do you like practicing? (No response) I don't think she really knows why she has given up. I think it's partly, it's a good expression of what she overall feels about anything now. And that is, 'what's the use?'

MOTHER 146: Well she did real good in her music and we were so pleased with her.

PASTOR 147: But supposing I try and try hard to play piano and play it well. What would you feel, Mary, if you practiced well and had lessons well in hand, would you feel that your parents would want you to play a little bit better?

MARY 148: Just a little bit more all the time.

PASTOR 149: Just a little bit more. So, 'why try?' I think this is the bind you're in.

The mother continues to resist but the father rejoins the pastor:

MOTHER 150: Well, we didn't give up the piano lessons until I talked with the teacher first (all talking).

FATHER 151: But that's not the basic point . . . No, that's not the basic point.

PASTOR 151: Well, but you're . . . , it doesn't matter what the teacher decided, she was through way, way back.

MOTHER 152: Well, she was through months before we stopped her. (Yes.) But on the other hand, Mary wanted me to sit right beside her while she practiced every note, and if she made a mistake and I corrected her, then she did not like that. And yet, in having had a little bit of music, I could not sit there and let her play the same note wrong every time . . .

FATHER 153: This isn't a matter of actuality, this is a matter of feelings.

MOTHER 154: Yes, but I think you've got to understand why she feels—I think this all carries out why she feels she's not good enough.

But the father, too, has difficulty seeing his role in creating his high expectations and the mother catches a glimpse.

FATHER 155: The point is, how do we show Mary we don't expect this out of her. That I have never asked for anything on her report card but S's . . . if she gets a G, fine. If she gets an E, fine. But I've never been disappointed that she doesn't get G's. It's just that, I, in my own way of thinking, maybe I'm wrong, but the only way you'll get anything is to give a little something . . . either of yourself or what it is . . . that you can't set a goal here and then reach this goal without setting a goal a little bit farther. Now if you're going to take one breath, you'll die . . . you've got to take another breath. You've got to go on and it's not that we're criticizing Mary, it's, and I don't frankly know how to show her that I don't want everything out of her, I just want her to be . . .

PASTOR 156: Well, I think that is at work here that could be helpful—I sense within you and perhaps it's within both of you, as parents, a feeling that you have to help her strive to be better and set goals beyond what she has done as her next, her next task.

FATHER 157: Oh no, not really. It may sound that way, but if she never was the greatest piano player in the world, it wouldn't bother me a bit . . .

PASTOR 158: No, wait a minute. No. I'm not talking about your setting goals way beyond her, you want to set them a *little bit* beyond . . .

MOTHER 159: . . . keep moving them up just a little bit more.

PASTOR 160: You are saying, if she does this much, then I know she can do that and I have a right to expect that she could with growth and practice and effort be a little bit better . . .

FATHER 161: . . . grow, yes . . .

PASTOR 162: Yes, now what I think you are saying is that you feel this is your responsibility to set the sights. Now what I sense is the deep disappointment in Mary is that she can't set her own sights—and she does. We like to grow ourselves and we like to feel we are pleasing others and surprising our parents with what we can do. And she doesn't get a chance to surprise you ever with what she can do; and to please you with what she came up with. Because you feel the need to help her, and to her next level, and this not only doesn't help her enjoy the full measure of accomplishment at this moment in this level, but it doesn't give this mechanic within herself, the thrust within herself, to . . .' I'll make the next effort and this will please them.' Now, Mary wants to please. As deeply as any child. And would want to please in these very directions you would want to be pleased by.

The mother who seemed to be grasping her role in setting higher demands now puzzles about another situation in which she doesn't see this. This time the father comes back in and sees the point.

MOTHER 163: Well, I have a question. Now why—now I will not cook with Mary any more. I have all the things for her and I am very happy when she does make something. In fact, I would like for her to make something every Saturday, nothing would please me more. And I always have it on hand. I cannot cook with Mary and I can't do many things with Mary, because when we get to doing something, having majored in Home Ec., I'm far from being the best, but I feel that I do know a few of the rules along the way that I want to give these to Mary, and then let her work them out the way she thinks is best. But what I run into, is immediately—perhaps my way of trying to help her is not correct and there is a wall right here. I want to give her suggestions on the way to do it, and help her so that the next time she will say, 'Well now I have done this and I know that to make a level teaspoon, take a knife and take it off, and that's a level teaspoonful.' I am trying to give Mary all this and she doesn't want it. 'I want to do it my way, I don't want to do it that way.' And so you see, I feel like I'm being pushed back; and yet she wants you to work with her. When it was her music, she wanted me to sit right there while she practiced. If she is going to make something, she wants you to be there while she makes it. This is fine, except you see, we get into such a hassle, that I feel it's not good for Mary and it's not good for me to stand there and argue with her about something, so I say, 'all right, you do it yourself,' and of course, I know that many times she gets into trouble because she doesn't know what to do. But, I feel like I can't help her. I want to help her, but apparently I'm going about it the wrong way.

PASTOR 164:   Well, I sense a real concern for her making *good* cherry pies . . . or whatever . . . because there are certain ways you can louse up making cherry pies.

MOTHER 165:   Well, I don't want her to be disappointed in her efforts . . .

PASTOR 166:   Well . . .

MOTHER 167:   . . . and she won't know how to do it if someone doesn't give her a little bit of help.

PASTOR 168:   All right. Then you're just documenting you have a real concern for her making good cherry pies. Now, the thing you do know, you're not ready to do is to be happy about making mud pies.

MOTHER 169:   (Astonished.) Well, we eat everything she makes regardless of whether it's good or not and she won't touch it. So I don't know whether you'd say that or not.

PASTOR 170:   We're not talking about the eating. We're talking about the process. I don't think you enjoy a mud pie for all the zest and enthusiasm of putting oneself into it that you can do.

MOTHER 171:   Well, probably not, because it was pushed into me at school, that you do things right or wrong, and that you should do it right.

PASTOR 172:   That there's just one way to do things! And if you do things by one way you miss all the fun in life that comes by making mud pies.

MOTHER 173:   Well, maybe I didn't make any mud pies when I was little, or very few of them, let's put it that way.

PASTOR 174:   Possibly, or (Father: That's a wonderful way of putting it) the real problem is that there is a deep joy that can never be had later in life and can only be had right now in not being perfect, in not making pies, just making mud pies. This being a pretend stance. One of the deep things, deep things that Mary is looking for—and this is why she wants you along side of her right now and this is all she should be getting out of cooking right now—and that is a sense of, this is a joy that a woman has and will have some sense of delight from her husband because she does it well. And a boy can do this? Sure. But he'll be, he'll be an oddball if he does. So this is not available to him. The unique kind of thing that Mary is picking up; this is part of what it means to be a woman. And what she does is drastically insignificant compared to whether there is joy in standing in the kitchen and being like Mother. This is what wanting Mother around stands for.

FATHER 175:   Regardless of the product . . .

PASTOR 176:   Regardless of the product. This is the deeper learning that is going to be of so much fundamental value.

MOTHER 177: Then why ask for advice if you're not going to take it. (Father: Just for conversation) These are things that are hard for me to understand.

PASTOR 178: Just to talk . . . (The mother protests her difficulty in understanding further and then comes around.)

PASTOR 182: . . . But you see what I mean in terms of this.

MOTHER 183: Yes. Well you see. I didn't cook in the kitchen and as you brought out about the mud pies, I probably didn't make mud pies either. So, as I say, I know a lot of this is because I, the way I look on things and that's why I'm here. Because I want to see Mary's side of it as well as my own feeling on the matter.

The mother seems to acknowledge her part and her blindness in relation to Mary by her last statement. Her voice indicates an acceptance of the point that she had previously made in the first hour, namely, that "maybe we've set her standards too high." (58) The pastor then goes on to suggest that the way to reverse the vicious cycle which over-expectation has set in motion is through greater acceptance and appreciation of the feeble and inadequate attempts of the child. This will release her own desires to please for use in new trying rather than apathetic withdrawal.

FATHER 185: In other words, don't offer constructive criticism. Forget it.

PASTOR 186: Yes. Support and accept. Support what's been done and accept.

MOTHER 187: But support it enthusiastically when you don't feel it? I mean, I'm a very honest person clear down to my toes and I don't say, 'Yes, it's nice.' And it is nice, but I can't get all this exuberance and softness that is not there. I don't do it with anyone.

PASTOR 188: But then this is exactly (Father: your problem), yes, your problem. You're not seeing what there is from her point of view that represents something to be exuberant about.

The child joins in to document the mother's frank and candid behavior and absence of the pleasant niceties:

MARY 197:   If they say, 'How do I look in it?' (a dress). You say, 'You look funny.'

MOTHER 198:   No, I don't say that, but as I say, the truth has been so instilled in me that I can't do all this fancy stuff when I know it's not right.

FATHER 199:   Well, that's what he's saying. This is our problem and we've got to practice with it.

PASTOR 200:   Well, there are all levels of truth, you see, I think this is what you have to be willing to accept . . . is that there is a truth of the accomplishment of the 11-year-old, or the 3-year old, or the 5-year old, in its sense of rightness and appropriateness . . . there's a truth in it, that you just can't get at any other age point and this is the *truthness,* the rightness. That it is the achievement, the product of the level of this ability and this level of maturity.

MOTHER 201:   But I am not an exuberant person.

PASTOR 202:   And it's not the truth of adult perfection—and yet it's the truth, I mean—mud pies are really wonderful things and I can't get back to making them again. I couldn't make a mud pie to save my soul. I'm spoiled into adulthood, and yet the exuberance of a 3-year old about a mud pie is something to behold. It's a real truth. This is an accomplishment. It's the stuff—rather than say, 'Oh, don't waste your time on mud' —it's the stuff out of which Empire State Buildings are made. If a 3-year old can construct this, then a 4-year old can make a better mud pie. And this says to each age, its own level. You really have to be willing to appreciate its own inner sense of meaning; its own sense of rightness, that must be there.

FATHER 203:   Understanding the others' viewpoint.

PASTOR 204:   Now I would suggest that if you make this kind of effort with Mary, on this day to day thing with school, jobs, etc., she'll be so startled that she'll get a whole new zest and enthusiasm in life for trying to do things that are startling to you because she'll realize there are some things—you will have broken through her expectation that nothing is going to be right. And she'll be free to go ahead in discovering something that will be even more pleasing. Let's try this for a while and maybe two or three months from now you let me know about it. Then we'll have another session about three months from now. And if things are going well, why we'll skip it; and if not, we'll have another session. OK?

FATHER: Umhmm.
            (Session concludes.)

There are three matters worthy of note in this latter half of the family session. First, the points of interpretation about role conflicts which the pastor makes are essentially matters which previously each parent has come to on his own. They are not strange or mysterious judgments from on high. Though the pastor's role becomes didactic at times, it is interpretation and teaching within the horizon of the awareness presented by the parents. Whether this is pure "reflection of feelings" or pure "interpretation" seems not to be the issue. Within the understanding of persons as interacting social agents, the work of the pastor helps each to be a more responsible person to the other and to include in greater awareness certain perceptions already held dimly.

Secondly we note that the parents' understanding of their own agency in regard to the unsatisfactory responses from their daughter pulses like an alternating current. First the light glows to one, then to another. In effect the three-way conversation between pastor, father and mother becomes a kind of dialogue. The pastor with mother sees what the father does not perceive at the moment. Then the pastor with father sees what the mother does not perceive at the moment. Out of this comes the prospect of continued talk to each other by the father and mother without the pastor in which each help supplement the awareness of the other.

Thirdly, the child's own agency and responsibility in relation to the parents is dealt with realistically too. While the primary concern is to facilitate parental understanding of their part in the family problem, the child is not exempt from a responsible participation in whatever has been the difficulty.

The upshot of this session is that the pastor has entered briefly but strategically into the world of this family. Having noted the various ways in which each regard others and self he proceeds to help relate the points of discrepancy in role perceptions to the points of difficulty in the family relationship. An effort toward greater role congruity has been made. Then having done this much he steps back from the family, leaving to them the responsibility for their continued life and work with each other. To the child, he accords some means of appraising the whole situation in terms of its interpersonal complexities. At the very least the child is assured that family problems are *family* problems. The inclination to scapegoat parental needs for perfection and success into the problem of a child who is "beyond the normal" is checked. Parental fears of a "wild teenager" are checked. Parental lack of understanding is clearly brought forward as a parental lack. All the problems of family living are not resolved by this one session. But the family is helped to see that theirs is a mutual responsibility for whatever problems they may have.

There is a very real danger in a complex emotional situation such as a family counseling session that the pastor will lose his objective-empathic perspective and become a protagonist for a cause. The cause could be hidden. There may be residues of reaction to parental authority left behind from his own adolescence. Or he may respond to the child in terms of remnants of his own child-self, seeking through this child before him what he once desired for himself. These or similar counter-transference problems are easily activated in a family session. Hence the pastor needs to be especially sensitive to the issue of his own objectivity. Trying to stay within the phenomenal awareness of parents and child while bringing points of role discrepancy into the open is a work that needs to be done gingerly. Where the counselor moves outside of parental awareness he should be ready to drop the point if resistance occurs. The resistance in the above session alternated from parent to parent and thus never became an outright barrier to further thinking and discovery.

The one way by which the pastor may know he is remaining objective is that he has acquired a warm "feel" for the situation of both the parents and the child. If he finds he cannot enter fully into both the parents' and the child's shoes, then his helpfulness will have begun to evaporate. At such a point halting the session and buying time through scheduling another session in a week will provide leeway for consulting with someone over one's own entanglements.

It should be noted that the suggestion of further sessions is entirely dependent upon the degree of resolution and congruence which is achieved in a single session. Follow-up by a pastoral call after a two or three week lapse might be the simplest way to see if the family itself is working things through any better. When using the parish call to follow-up, sensitivity to whether they are in need of more help or more time alone is important. The shift of initiative from the family to the pastor should be only a temporary and casual one. Respect for the other as persons means initiating the parish call in a casual way and avoiding pressing for exploration of any issue until the family's readiness to seek further help is clear. When one discovers in a call that all is going well, this is enough.

It is perfectly appropriate to close a family session with open prayer when this is a natural idiom for a family. Though the session above was with a church family open prayer was not used. The language of prayer was judged to be present covertly in the relationship of helpfulness and in the family's searching for better understanding.

The family returns to status of one of the parish families seen in various activities, programs and worship after a family counseling session. After an initial follow-up call, then further parish calling need not be pressed as an exception to usual practice. The channels of communication between the family and pastor return to the ordinary contacts of parish life.

A PASTORAL THEOLOGICAL POSTSCRIPT

The impression could easily be gained from the foregoing chapters of Part Two that the pastor's work with the family in the family counseling session is the whole of the pastor's relationship. This we must now correct. It should not be assumed that a single session brings such a burst of insight that the parents are never again perplexed. For the moment they are helped, but they continue to meet the mystifying and the baffling in their relationship with their daughter as the early teen years come on. Four years later they again feel the need of some counsel and again meet the suggestion of facing the question as a family. The one session certainly does not solve everything or dramatically change the terms of their existence. It is a help. But what we have seen so far has its limitations.

The family counseling case in Chapters Five and Six has been offered as an example of extraordinary pastoral care, the care extended by the pastor to the special circumstances of the individual—in this instance to the family. What we have seen thus far indicates a creative way to enter into the problem situation of a family and achieve some clarification in the relationships of each to the other. What we have presented to this point deserves to be considered *care*, but can we say that it is *pastoral* care? If pastoral is limited to the functions of the shepherd, then the answer is yes. At the functional level shepherding, caring and pastoring then become synonymous. That kind of caring which bridges divisions and effects better understanding between family members is pastoral caring. But if pastoral refers to the ministry of Christ offered through his life, death and resurrection, then the *pastoral* dimension of care in this family session is still attenuated. Pastoral care in this sense is a message of God's reconciliation in Christ as well as a ministry of human love to a neighbor.

For the message of Christ's life, death and resurrection to be fully expressed in pastoral care, the human situation needs to be seen in its cry of insufficiency, perversity and contradiction. When this happens the limits of our ability to save ourselves from the ambiguities of life begin to be appreciated. Then the Word of Grace which has been spoken in Christ begins to speak to the depth of the human plight. When one is grasped by this truth then the response of faith further requires faithfulness in our ministry to others.

The meaning of this message to the Betterly family and to the situation in which they find themselves would need to be explored in order to say that our pastoral care to the family is complete. The message of God's work of salvation in Christ is only adumbrated with the family in the midst of their encounter with the limitations, finitude and sinfulness of their humanity. Within this encounter the meaning of grace offered to man in his sinfuless can be quickened and with it faith in what is God's act of gracious forgiveness toward our sinning.

An approximation of the discovery of their finitude and of the limitation of their own resources is found by the Betterlys in their acknowledgement of the need for help. In one sense the pastor misses the opportunity to lift up the deeper reference and significance of this moment of frustration as the kind of moment in which the need for grace is made clear. In another sense the pastor's approach of helping the family to explore the problem of their life together more fully is the beginning of the awareness that ministries of reconciliation may symbolize the great message of reconciliation which we have in Christ.

A further level of the character of the sin of our being is opened up in the section running from statement 114 to statement 121 found at the opening of Chapter Seven. At this point the parents through the mother acknowledge the kind of self-defeating circle of expectations and attitudes in which they are caught along with the daughter. Again the pastoral response is one of caring as over against explicit reference to the message of God's grace toward us. There is an implicit assumption in what follows that insight and understanding will rescue this family from their plight. There is an attempt to open awareness, broaden understanding and help each to see the other in terms of the other's own self-perspection.

What is not captured at this moment is the clue to the human situation as it is before the grace of God. What is not seized is the fact that as we begin to see the bankruptcy of our own resourcefulness, we become ready to hear the word which God has spoken. Perhaps the pastoral approach of the particular moment is enough to achieve a level of greater understanding of the ambiguity of the situation of parents, children, and a family. The good which we would do, we do not; that which we would not, we do. The perversity of the human heart is seen a little more fully and acknowledged. The ground has been prepared for speaking about the depth of human alienation and human contrariness. Certainly this aspect of the life of the Betterly's has been given a little deeper reality by the way in which they have looked and searched with the pastor the situation in which they stand. The prelude has occurred. Now the pastor has the opportunity in some future moment to explore one further matter. This is the way in which the ambiguity of our being, the limitations of our own goodness and the finitude of our own vision spell out the need which we have for the word which God has spoken in Jesus Christ. The pastoral conversation has moved through one level only until this further word is spoken. The timing of the pastoral disclosure of the fuller human situation and the way it stands judged and forgiven by God is not programmatic. In a sense the fact that further difficulties were to be encountered by the Betterlys could have provided the occasion for linking the recurrence with a constant in the human situation, namely our sinfulness—our missing the mark over and over again.

This pastoral theological postscript permits our clarifying that pastoral care with the Betterlys has not been completed in the family session as recorded and presented. In effect the end of the counseling session enjoins upon the family the necessity of their walking in love—in greater care for and understanding of each other—without any mention of the relation of this commandment to the grace which God has offered to the tragic inability of men to walk by love. It is thus a misleading and deceptive departure which they take of the pastor at this point. The parents believe that they must try harder; that they must practice a little more keeping their problem from intruding upon the child. The point is not that their efforts to walk with greater understanding are inappropriate. But walking with love as though it were a simple possibility means that the family—especially the parents—have not yet been helped to see the impossible aspects of the commandment of love. They have not come to see their need for forgiveness is as deep and far-reaching as their ingenuity in being good parents. They have not yet faced the reality of the ambiguous good and evil which is entwined in all human life. They have not yet seen the depth of the need for grace. They have not yet felt the depth of God's judgment upon the best of efforts. As a consequence they have not yet heard the fullness of God's work of forgiveness as spoken to them in the midst of this situation.

As the Betterlys take leave of the pastor the level reached is one of clearing the air and of facing some of the complicities of their own being in the problems which confound them. But the pastor should not take leave of them. He should await and seek the moment when the truth of their human situation can come clearer at another level —the level of human ambiguity which knows that man cannot save himself. This is the level on which God's judgment and grace speak. This is the level on which acts of love toward others become transformed because they are responses to the love with which we have been loved. The walk of the Christian is then by faith not by a program of self-improvement and human betterment. The sure reality of human sin is appreciated as the demonic powers which dwell in every phase of our being. It is from the grasp of such resident powers of our being that we need to be rescued constantly through the grace of God.

A SELECTED BIBLIOGRAPHY

I Congregational Care with Families

SURVEYS OF MENTAL ILLNESS

1. Gerald Gurin, Joseph Veroff, and Sheila Feld, *Americans View Their Mental Health*, New York: Basic Books, Inc., 1960.

2. Leo Srole, et al., *Mental Health in the Metropolis: The Midtown Manhattan Study*, Vol. I, New York: McGraw-Hill Book Company, Inc., 1962.

3. A. B. Hollingshead, and F. C. Redlich, *Social Class and Mental Illness*, New York: John Wiley & Sons, Inc., 1958.

4. Richard McCann, *The Churches and Mental Health*, New York: Basic Books, Inc., 1962.

5. Dorothea Leighton, et al., *The Character of Danger*, New York: Basic Books, Inc., 1963.

THE CRISIS OF INTIMACY

6. John Dollard, Frank Auld, and Alice M. White, *Steps in Psychotherapy*, New York: The Macmillan Company, 1953.

7. Abram Kardiner, *The Psychological Frontiers of Society*, New York: Columbia University Press, 1945.

8. James West, *Plainville, USA*, New York: Columbia University Press, 1945.

9. Gibson Winter, *Love and Conflict*, Garden City: Doubleday & Company, Inc., 1958.

10. Henry A. Grunwald, Editor, *Sex in America*, New York: Bantam Books, Inc., 1964.

11. Bruno Bettleheim, and Morris Janowitz, *Social Change and Prejudice,* New York: The Free Press of Glencoe, 1964.

12. Harry Stack Sullivan, *The Interpersonal Theory of Psychiatry,* New York: W. W. Norton and Company, Inc., 1953.

13. Winston Ehrmann, *Premarital Dating Behavior,* New York: Holt, Rinehart & Winston, Inc., 1959.

14. Nathan W. Ackerman, "Behavior Trends and Disturbances of the Contemporary Family," in I. Galdston, Editor, *The Family in Contemporary Society,* New York: International Universities Press, 1958.

To Help Parents

15. Sidonie Matsner Gruenberg, Editor, *The Encyclopedia of Child Care and Guidance,* Garden City: Doubleday & Company, Inc.

16. John Levy, and Ruth Monroe, *The Happy Family,* New York: Alfred A. Knopf, Inc., 1938.

17. Benjamin Spock, *The Pocket Book of Baby and Child Care,* New York: Pocket Books, Inc., 1946.

18. Helen A. Sherrill, *Christian Parenthood,* Richmond: John Knox Press, 1965.

19. Margaret Ribble, *The Rights of Infants,* New York: Columbia University Press, 1943.

20. Margaret Ribble, *The Personality of the Young Child,* New York: Columbia University Press, 1954.

The Family's Purposes

21. William F. Kenkel, *The Family in Perspective,* New York: Appleton-Century-Crofts, Inc., 1960.

22. Arthur R. Calhoun, *A Social History of the Family,* Vol. I, Colonial Period, New York: Barnes & Noble, Inc., 1960.

23. Daniel R. Miller, and Guy E. Swanson, *The Changing American Parent,* New York: John Wiley & Sons, Inc., 1958.

24. Ernest W. Burgess, Harvey J. Locke, and Mary M. Thomes, *The Family from Institution to Companionship,* 3rd Edition, New York: American Book Company, 1963.

25. Roger Mehl, *Society and Love, Ethical Problems of Family Life*, Philadelphia: The Westminster Press, 1964.

PASTORAL CARE AND SMALL GROUPS

26. Carl R. Rogers, *On Becoming a Person*, Boston: Houghton Mifflin Company, 1961.

27. Wayne, Oates, *Protestant Pastoral Counseling*, Philadelphia: The Westminster Press, 1962.

28. Robert A. Raines, *New Life in the Church*, New York: Harper & Row, Publishers, 1961.

29. John L. Casteel, Editor, *Spiritual Renewal Through Personal Groups*, New York: Association Press, 1957.

30. David P. McPhail, Editor, *Union Seminary, Quarterly Review*, March, 1961, Volume XVI, No. 3, "Renewal in the Churches."

31. Tom Allan, *The Face of My Parish*, London: SCM Press Ltd., 1954.

32. Elizabeth O'Conner, *The Call to Commitment*, New York: Harper & Row, Publishers, 1963.

33. Joseph W. Knowles, *Group Counseling*, Englewood Cliffs, N.J.: Prentice-Hall, Inc., 1964.

34. Philip A. Anderson, *Church Meetings that Matter*, Philadelphia: Christian Education Press, 1965.

35. Robert C. Leslie, Guest Editor, "Small Groups in the Church," *Pastoral Psychology*, Vol. 15, No. 145, June, 1964.

36. Robert A. Edgar, "The Listening Structured Group" in (35).

37. Sara Little, *Learning Together in the Christian Fellowship*, Richmond: John Knox Press, 1956.

38. John R. Fry, *A Hard Look at Adult Christian Education*, Philadelphia: The Westminster Press, 1961.

THE MISSION OF GOD'S PEOPLE

39. George W. Webber, *The Congregation in Mission*, Nashville: Abingdon Press, 1964.

40. Arnold Come, *Agents of Reconciliation*, Philadelphia: The Westminster Press, 1960.

41. Colin Williams, *Where in the World*, New York: Central Committee on Evangelism, National Council of Churches, 1963.

42. Robert Spike, *In But Not of the World*, New York: Association Press, 1957.

II Family Counseling

PERSONS IN FAMILIES

43. Ernest Jones, *The Life and Work of Sigmund Freud*, 3 volumes, New York: Basic Books, Inc., 1953–1957.

44. Percival J. Symonds, *The Ego and the Self*, New York: Appleton-Century-Crofts, 1951.

45. Harry Stack Sullivan, *The Interpersonal Theory of Psychiatry*, New York: W. W. Norton & Company, Inc., 1953.

46. George Herbert Mead, *Mind, Self and Society*, Chicago: University of Chicago Press, 1934.

47. Walter J. Garre, *Basic Anxiety*, New York: Philosophical Library, Inc., 1962.

48. Robert D. Hess, and Gerald Handel, *Family Worlds*, Chicago: University of Chicago Press, 1959.

49. Walter Toman, *Family Constellations*, New York: Springer Publishing Company, Inc., 1961.

50. N. W. Bell, and E. F. Vogel, "The Emotionally Disturbed Child as the Family Scapegoat," in N. W. Bell and E. F. Vogel, Editors, *The Family*, New York: The Free Press of Glencoe, 1960.

51. Samuel Liebman, Editor, *Emotional Forces in the Family*, Philadelphia: J. B. Lippincott Co., 1959.

PERSONS IN MARRIAGES

52. Victor W. Eisenstein, Editor, *Neurotic Interaction in Marriage*, New York: Basic Books, Inc., 1956.

53. Robert F. Winch, *Mate-Selection*, New York: Harper & Row, Publishers, 1958.

54. R. Lofton Hudson, *Marital Counseling*, Englewood Cliffs, N.J.: Prentice-Hall, Inc., 1963.

55. Harry F. Tashman, *The Marriage Bed, An Analyst's Casebook*, New York: Ace Books, Inc., 1959. A broad, interpretive point of view explores many kinds of dyadic relationships in marriages using case material as an auxiliary rather than an exclusive focus.

FAMILY COUNSELING

56. Julia Jessie Taft, *Family Case-Work and Counseling*, Philadelphia: University of Pennsylvania Press, 1948.

57. C. F. Midelfort, *The Family and Psychotherapy*, New York: McGraw-Hill Book Company, 1957.

58. Nathan W. Ackerman, *The Psychodynamics of Family Life*, New York: Basic Books, Inc., 1958.

59. "The Emergence of Family Psychotherapy Upon the Present Scene" in Morris Stein, Editor, *Contemporary Psychotherapies*, New York: The Free Press of Glencoe, 1960.

60. Erika Chance, *Families in Treatment*, New York: Basic Books, Inc., 1959.

61. Don D. Jackson, "Family Interaction, Family Homeostasis and Some Implications for Conjoint Family Psychotherapy" in Jules Masserman, Editor, *Individual and Familial Dynamics*, New York: Grune and Stratton, Inc., 1959.

62. "Family Therapy in the Family of the Schizophrenic" in Morris Stein, Editor, *Contemporary Psychotherapies*, New York: The Free Press of Glencoe, 1960.

63. "Monad, Dyad and the Family Therapy of Schizophrenics," in A. Burton, Editor, *Psychotherapy of the Psychoses*, New York: Basic Books, Inc., 1961.

64. Martin Grotjahn, *Psychoanalysis and the Family Neurosis*, New York: W. W. Norton & Company, Inc., 1960.

65. Nathan Ackerman, F. L. Beatman, and S. Sanford, Editors, *Exploring the Base for Family Therapy*, New York: Family Service Association, 1961.

66. Theodore Lidz, *The Family and Human Adaptation,* New York: International Universities Press, 1963.

67. Jan Ehrenwald, *Neurosis in the Family and Patterns of Psychosocial Defense,* New York: Harper & Row, Publishers, 1963.

68. Virginia Satir, *Conjoint Family Therapy,* Palo Alto, California: Science and Behavior Books, Inc., 1964.

69. Charles Stewart, *The Minister as Marriage Counselor,* Nashville: Abingdon Press, 1961.

III   Theology and Pastoral Care

70. Daniel D. Williams, *The Minister and the Care of Souls,* New York: Harper & Row, Publishers, 1961.

71. Eduard Thurneysen, *A Theology of Pastoral Care,* Richmond: John Knox Press, 1962.

72. Edward E. Thornton, *Theology and Pastoral Counseling,* Englewood Cliffs, N.J.: Prentice-Hall, Inc., 1964.

73. Paul Tillich, *Systematic Theology,* Volume III, Chicago: University of Chicago Press, 1964.

INDEX

AUTHORS

Ackerman, Nathan, 73, **79**
Adler, Alfred, 68, 71
Anderson, Philip, 40
Anderson, Phoebe, 40

Chance, Erika, 72
Come, Arnold, 34

Edgar, Robert A., 40

Fairchild, Roy W., 21
Freud, Sigmund, 18, 65
Fromm, Erich, 67
Fry, John R., 29, 42

Garre, Walter, 72
Grothjan, Martin, 73

Handel, Gerald, 72
Hess, Robert D., 72
Horney, Karen, 67
Hunt, Morton M., 20

Jackson, Don D., 74

Kardiner, Abram, 18, **19**
Kinsey, Alfred, 18

Lidz, T., 74
Löhe, Wilhelm, 34

McNeill, John T., 34
Mead, George Herbert, 69
Midelfort, C. F., 73

Niles, D. T., 54

O'Conner, Elizabeth, 30

Ribble, Margaret, 23
Rogers, Carl R., 7, 25, 26

Satir, Virginia, 73
Spock, Benjamin, 21
Sullivan, Harry Stack, 18, 67, 68
Symonds, Percival, 67

Thurneysen, Eduard, 35
Toman, Walter, 72

Warkentin, John, 71
West, James, 18
Wynn, John C., 21

SUBJECTS

Adult study, 56
Anxiety, interpersonal, 68

Caring, 25
Concern group
    cautions, 56 ff.
    concerns, 41

Concern group (*Cont.*)
initiating, 45–49
observer, 50
overseeing, 45 ff.
resource meeting, 50, 60
values, 41 ff. 51–53
Church of Our Saviour, 30
Church Structure
defects, 36–38
new, 38 ff.
Congruence, 25, 78 ff., 80
Conversation, Christian, 54

Discipline
church, 35, 56, 58
group, 26, 38

Empathy, 25, 131
Equipping ministry, 38 ff.

Family
conjugal, 15
constellation, 70 ff.
functions, 26 ff.
in Christ, 44 ff.
therapy, 73 ff.

Glenview Community Church, 6, 40

House Church, 53

Incongruity, 77 ff., 81, 87

Intimacy
crisis, 14 ff.
training in, 20, 42

Lay apostolate, 53 ff.
Leadership, shared, 51 ff.

Middle-class, success, 114 ff.
Mission, nurture for, 29 ff.
Mobility, residential, 15

Parental insight, 79 ff.
Parenthood, crisis of, 21 ff.
Pastoral Care
congregational, 37 ff.
extraordinary, 34, 132
lay role, 6, 24, 36, 51, 87, 88
ordinary, 33
pastor's family, 61
Personality theory, 63 ff.

Reconciliation
message, 33, 133
ministry, 33, 133
rehearsal for, 55 ff.
training in, 85

Self, 67 ff.
Style of Life, Christian, 29, 58

Tape Recording, 88
Theological reflection, 55, 132 ff.
Therapists, natural, 52, 59

This volume provides a whole new dimension in counseling procedures, showing creative and tested methods for counseling the family as a unit. It covers the three vital areas: general ministries to the family as a family, supportive ministries of mutual pastoral care and family counseling.

Some of the areas discussed are: child disturbances . . . marriage relations . . . the role of the church in bringing together its family-church activities . . . the family under stress . . . parent-child relationships . . . the importance of the pastor's home visits . . . family festivals, camping and fellowship activities.

Also included is a full verbatim study of a family-group case focusing on the specific need and the actual therapy.

Here, then, is a creative, tested, analyzed application of modern pastoral care principles for both cases of crisis and non-crisis.

THE AUTHOR

Dr. Russell J. Becker is the Associate Professor of Pastoral Theology at Yale Divinity School. A United Church of Christ minister, he is a member of various professional societies and served from 1958-1962 as a member of the Executive Council of the American Academy of Psychotherapists. He has written numerous articles for religious and professional journals.

Dr. Russell L. Dicks was General Editor for the Successful Pastoral Counseling series until the time of his death in March, 1965. A pioneer in pastoral counseling, Dr. Dicks was Director of the Central Florida Counseling Center in Orlando, Florida. For nearly 30 years he trained hundreds of clergymen who are now successfully engaged in counseling throughout the churches of America.